THE THREE WORLDS

OF

Albert Schweitzer

~~~ **ROBERT PAYNE** ~~~

THE THREE WORLDS
OF

Albert Schweitzer

THOMAS NELSON & SONS

Edinburgh   **NEW YORK**   *Toronto*

FOR

Ivy Wilson AND *Gorham Munson*

AFFECTIONATELY

~~~ Contents ~~~

THE THREE WORLDS

OF

Albert Schweitzer

~~~ 1 ~~~
Africa the Nightmare

OF ALL THE CONTINENTS
Africa is the oldest, the one which has been cultivated for
the longest time, the one with the most ancient history.
Deeply ingrown in the African mind is the consciousness of
an ancient past: of kings who died long ago and whose
names are forgotten, of empires which stretched across the
continent and whose capitals have vanished. The first stir-
rings of civilization were in Africa on the shores of the
Nile. Once great arts flourished in Benin and great fortresses
were built at Zimbabwe, but we know neither the names of
the builders of the fortresses nor the names of the artists
who modelled the superb sculptured heads of Benin. A
strange anonymity hovers over the ancient land.

Perhaps it was inevitable. There are innumerable reasons
why the ancient African civilizations failed to survive and
why there were no written histories. In the gaunt and formidable immensity of Africa all men were nomads and their
civilizations seem to have been comparable to the rule of the
Scythians and the Tartar Hordes in Asia. There were great
cities, there was wealth, there were artists, but there was no

absorbing desire for permanence, no passionate determination to leave their mark on the earth. They lived inwardly, in a rhythm with the seasons, very close to the earth, which they worshipped, and they seem not to have cared overmuch for the things which Europeans cared for: comfort, order, mastery. So they became an easy prey to the freebooters who rounded the coasts of Africa. For four hundred years, from the fifteenth century to the nineteenth, their main contact with the West took place on slave-ships or on plantations or in the mines. They were a handsome and proud people, aware of their past, possessing a rich culture which satisfied their needs, content with their land, fearful of strangers. Confronted with the guns of Europeans and Americans, they submitted to overwhelming force. Now at last they have acquired guns of their own and they are determined to be rulers of their own land and to free Africa from colonialism. The revolt of Africa has begun.

Today Africa is in flames. From one end of the continent to the other the fire blazes, and it is too late to put it out. In South Africa, Kenya, Morocco, Tunisia, Algeria the white men are attempting to suppress the revolt of Africa by force of arms. It took no more than five years following the Second World War for the people of Asia to throw off the yoke of colonialism. Within another five years nearly all of Africa may be free. Meanwhile we pay in blood and treasure for the centuries of indignity the Africans have suffered at our hands.

The tragedy of course is that it need not have happened. There was no overwhelming reason why the colonial powers should have kept the Africans in bondage. If fifty years ago the Africans had been allowed the same rights as their western conquerors, if there had been no racial discrimination, if forced labor had not been demanded of them, if they had been given the same social advantages which even common laborers had gained, if they had been encouraged to become doctors and technicians and teachers and administrators instead of being forced into slavery or near-slavery, the violent explosion we are now witnessing would not have taken place, or it would have occurred in a form which could have been canalised into constructive ends. The bitterness lies deep. Today the armed African is in no mood to think clearly about his aims. He has acquired an anarchical taste for guerrilla warfare; he fights in Kenya in the same way that he fights in Algeria. He alone, with his handful of chosen companions, strikes against the invading power. So he avenges his honor, blindly raging against his colonial masters, in an anarchic desire to kill and efface the traces of colonialism. All too clearly it appears that before Africa is free there will be a blood-bath.

Nearly fifty years ago the great French missionary to the Sahara, Father de Foucauld, said: "If we do not bind these people to us, they will drive us away. Not only shall we lose the whole of the Empire, but the unity which we have given to it, and which it has for the first time since the world began, will turn against us: it will be hostile, dangerous and savagely against us." It is only in the last few years that we have learned how hostile, dangerous and savage can be the awakened anger of the African.

From the colonial officers came the myth that the African was uncivilized and could never except in the rarest instances become civilized. The missionaries were more tempted to see in the African a man they could study and learn from. They were surprised to discover that the black men possessed a profound, instinctive faith, possessed infinite patience under the most trying circumstances and lived deeply within himself in a strange rhythmic identification with the world around him—a quality which had almost disappeared in the strident advance of a mechanical century. When the history of Africa in the nineteenth century is written, it will not be sufficient to consult the explorers and the archives of the colonial powers. Hidden away in obscure parish magazines are the reports of obscure missionaries who wrote at length, and often brilliantly, of the lives of the black people they were attempting to convert. The French poet Charles Péguy wrote that the mystics construct, the politicians destroy. In Africa the missionaries often built edifices of faith which the colonial officers betrayed.

It is difficult for our generation to recapture the emotions of the early missionaries. For them Africa was not a Dark Continent, but a continent of intense and unfaltering light. For David Livingstone Africa was a land of infinite promise and delight. He enjoyed the company of Africans. He called himself "a dumpy sort of man with a Bible under his arm," and he was convinced that England possessed a divine mission in Africa. England would be the means by which the Africans would be brought to full maturity. More than anyone else he fought against the evils of slavery and made himself the spearhead of the attack upon slavery in the Indian Ocean. For him slavery was "this open sore of the world," and with a doctor's patience and a doctor's gift of healing he was determined to close the wound. Over and over again he insisted that commerce and education would eradicate the physical evils from which Africa was suffering, and that the African must be treated as an equal. He believed that Christianity was superior to all other religions, but he regarded the beliefs of the Africans with good humor and understanding. He was a Christian first, and explorer second, but exploring was part of his Christianity—he had an intense desire to bring all Africans to Christ, and if that meant traveling on foot through lands which had never been traveled by white men before, then he was prepared to travel until he dropped dead. He died at Ilala on his knees, as convinced as ever of the supreme importance of the tasks to which he had set his hand, and so great was the love and trust he had evoked among the black men, they carried his dead body from the heart of Africa to a place where the white men could receive it and give it proper burial. It took the Africans six months to discharge their self-imposed task. There have been few such triumphal marches in the known history of Africa.

Livingstone's bright Africa grew darker as the century came to an end. Soon the white men were everywhere, cutting down the forests, setting up trading posts along the rivers, quarreling over the corpse as jackals and leopards and vultures quarrel over the body of a dead hippopotamus. Seventeen years after Livingstone's death Joseph Conrad assumed command of a tiny river steamer in the upper Congo. He had no very clear idea why he was driven to take this command. He felt an inexplicable desire to explore the heart of Africa. He remained there for several months, nearly dying of fever and dysentery. Once he had to walk 200 miles through the forest to reach his ship. During the journey up-river he seemed to be moving slowly "on the edge of a black and incomprehensible frenzy." Some time later he encountered a company agent who became the model for Kurtz, the strange "megalomaniac and universal genius" who came out to Africa as "an emissary of pity, and science, and devil knows what else," only to die horribly cursing all Africans in a stagnant company station in the interior. In the end Kurtz, the idealist, oppressed by his own inner misery, became a murderer who killed the natives for the pure pleasure of decorating his fence-posts with their heads. His carefully reasoned argument against the Africans —all Africans—concludes with the words: "Exterminate all the brutes!" He represented a reversion to savagery which was not altogether uncommon among white men in Africa. As he lay dying, "he cried out in a whisper at some image, at some vision—he cried out twice, a cry that was no more than a breath: 'The horror! The horror!' The horror was there, and Marlow, who tells the story in *Heart of Darkness,* knew that it was of the white man's own making.

To survive in Africa at the turn of the century a white man needed qualities of heroism. The heat, the damp, the solitude—these were enemies worth a hero's passionate concern. Trader Horn snapped his fingers at the powers of darkness, and lived to tell the tale, though he embroidered it with stories of dark-skinned princesses. De Brazza, the French explorer who nearly succeeded in wresting the Congo from the King of the Belgians, behaved throughout his brief African career with astonishing gaiety. He possessed Livingstone's transparent goodness and good sense, and thought dangers existed to be overcome. The diaries of early Protestant missionaries in Equatorial Africa have biblical overtones: for them the steaming forests and the flooded rivers are Lands of Canaan, brimming with milk and honey. They died like flies, but faith uplifted them. "Before the Congo I was just a mere animal," Conrad said, and most of the missionaries would have agreed with him. Equatorial Africa with its unrelenting heat and terrifying strangeness was a challenge worth any man's best impulse. Here, if anywhere, a man could discover himself by submitting to the worst climate and the utmost rigors of nature. At that temperature, in those forests, a man walks by an inner light or he falls by the wayside.

When Albert Schweitzer went out to Africa, he was following in a great tradition. It is the custom now to regard missionaries with benevolent tolerance, but it was not so at the turn of the century. In those days missionaries—especially medical missionaries—were regarded as advance guards of civilization. They were the drummers of a new age. The newspapers, which reported the movements of Livingstone and sent Stanley to find him when he was lost, were also reporting at length on the activities of missionaries in India and China. Missions were fashionable, and a missionary returning to England or France was likely to be lionized. It is difficult for our generation to understand the importance attached to African missions in the days before Africa was completely colonized. Yet unless we do so we shall never understand the failure of the colonial powers nor why they occasionally succeeded so brilliantly. The problem of the missionaries lies at the heart of the colonial adventure in Africa.

Today Africa is a nightmare lit with feverish flames. This nightmare might not have happened if the colonial powers had studied carefully the example of the early missionaries, whose high purpose was to act as the cultural and spiritual arm of the colonizing power. But too soon these purposes were forgotten, or defeated by opposing sects of missionaries, and too often it was the megalomaniac, destructive Kurtz who achieved power.

When the Africans saw that the Europeans came without spiritual or cultural purposes, but were intent only on loot, they fought back. All over Africa there were these small hideous skirmishes between the Europeans armed with modern rifles and the Africans armed with spears and assagais. Inevitably the Europeans won; and in the colonies the Africans were enslaved or given only menial positions. Into the colonies were introduced economies which were to the advantage of the colonizing power and destructive to the economic life of the African, who was powerless to resist. They had no immunity to European diseases. The natives died off in epidemics of tuberculosis and syphilis. Their only refuge was to enter more deeply into themselves or into the terrifying world where the witch-doctor with his power over the invisible forces of nature reigned supreme.

By 1910 the humanitarian influence which had dominated the European colonists through much of the nineteenth century was on the wane. Few spoke up for the African. The colonial powers were out for loot, and in the process of acquiring loot were causing unimaginable suffering. Only here and there a few missionaries warned against the tragedy that was taking place. It was from these missionaries in French Equatorial Africa that Albert Schweitzer heard the story of the tragedy. He wrote in 1913, shortly after his arrival in Africa, explaining why he had given up his professorship at the University of Strasbourg, his literary work and his organ-playing in order to become a doctor serving the natives on the Ogowe River:

I had read about the physical miseries of the natives in the virgin forests: I had heard about them from missionaries, and the more I thought about it, the stranger it seemed to me that we Europeans trouble ourselves so little about the great humanitarian task which offers itself to us in far-off lands. The parable of Dives and Lazarus seemed to me to have been spoken directly to us! We are Dives, for, through the advances of medical science, we now know a great deal about disease and pain, and have innumerable means of fighting them: yet we take as a matter of course the incalculable advantage which this new wealth gives us! Out there in the colonies, however, sits wretched Lazarus, the colored folk, who suffers from illness and pain just as much as we do, nay, much more, and has absolutely no means of fighting them. And just as Dives sinned against the poor man at his gate because for want of thought he never put himself in his place and let his heart and conscience tell him what he ought to do, so do we sin against the poor man at our gate.[1]

What Schweitzer was saying was no more than Livingstone had said before him, but in the interval between them Africa had been carved up among the colonial powers and

[1] *On the Edge of the Primeval Forest.* By Albert Schweitzer. New York: The Macmillan Company. 1952.

was changed beyond recognition. Henceforward what had seemed simple to Livingstone was to prove unimaginably hard. Already the rot had set in, and the colonial powers were dedicated to a course which could only result in the loss of their colonial possessions.

It has been necessary to sketch in the background at some length to show that Schweitzer came to Africa at a critical moment in its history and to set him in his proper context. More than most missionaries he represented "the cultural and spiritual arm of the colonizing power." To an almost fantastic degree he possessed intellectual skills which he willingly sacrificed on behalf of the Africans. If he lacked Livingstone's profound affection for geography and exploration, he had explored singlehandedly vast regions of the human spirit. It is inconceivable that anyone could have been better equipped for the task before him. If by one man's example the course of colonization could have been changed, he could have done it. Himself a humanitarian rooted in the nineteenth century, he saw very early that the sins of the early colonists would have to be redeemed. Lazarus at war with Dives gives no quarter. And he was prepared, with all the strength in him, to see that the inevitable battle was fought as painlessly as possible.

By one of those accidents which seem to have been deliberately arranged, Schweitzer chose to come to Africa at a critical moment, just before the First World War showed the Africans that the colonial powers were hopelessly divided among themselves. By a similar accident Schweitzer chose as the field of his endeavor a hot steamy insalubrious region inhabited by tribes which had only recently been

fighting among themselves over a rich slave-market controlled by the Portuguese. On the Ogowe river in the Gabon
Territory of French Equatorial Africa lived the remnants of
eight once powerful tribes, decimated by disease. "We are
all sick people here," a native told Schweitzer shortly after
his arrival. On the banks of the Ogowe, in the dank forests
stretching into the hinterland, all the ills of Africa seemed
to be concentrated.

In this savage world man seems an interloper. He has not
the claws and teeth of the carnivores. He cannot fly like a
bird, run like a deer, climb like a monkey. Rooted to the
earth, he has not the immense strength nor the striking
power of snakes, nor can he go like them for weeks without
food. In equatorial Africa only one animal is admirably
fitted to live and survive the sweltering heat. This is the
hippopotamus, which feeds and sleeps in the shady forest
at night and spends its days standing in the river with only
its nostrils showing above the water.

When the abrupt tropical night drops over the forest, men
are blinded by the darkness and deafened by the strange
roars, grunts, squeaks and slithering sounds of the forest
animals. The forest gives off its exhalations and seems to
breathe. For long months on the Ogowe the darkness at night
is total, for the moon is hidden behind clouds. In such a land
men come easily to the belief that the night is haunted and
the ghosts of the night must be appeased. Taboos are legion,
and the fetish doctors with their powerful ju-jus are believed
to hold converse with the elemental powers. Divine strength
pours through them. With a glance, with a pointed finger,
with a wish they can cause the death of a man: so the natives

believe even now. To ward off the evil spirits the fetish doctors prepare amulets which they sell at outrageous prices.
All natives wear these amulets; they hang them up in their
huts, place them near their beds, set them up wherever they
are working and carry them about their bodies. A family
might have ten or fifteen amulets to protect it from different
evils. There are amulets for good fortune, amulets to ward
off lightning, one amulet to protect a man hunting and another to protect him when he returns home. A small leather
bag, a buffalo horn, a fruit-seed which has been hollowed
out will be filled with dead leaves, pieces of metal, red
feathers, a leopard's claw, a splinter from a mirror. The best
and biggest fetishes contain pieces of a human skull from a
man or woman killed expressly to provide the fetish. There
are special fetishes to be worn by mothers at childbirth, by
babies at the moment they are born and by babies at wean-
ing-time. A man suffering sickness will demand loudly that
his fetish come to his aid; if it fails, it is the sign that a new
and more powerful one is needed. Schweitzer himself inherited, and kept, a fetish containing two fragments of a human
skull.

Driven by fear, subject to sudden inexplicable moments of
panic which occur most often in the middle of the night, at
the mercy of the fetish doctors, the natives live out their lives
in a fearful twilight of the imagination. Every object, every
gust of air, is magic, and all magic is evil, unless it comes in
contact in some way with a fetish. And because the fetish
doctors alone possess the power to make these protective
devices, they become themselves walking fetishes, sacred, to
be appeased as the evil spirits are appeased, never to be

molested even when they commit crimes. Recently, between
Libreville and Loango, it was discovered that between thirty
and forty people had been poisoned, dying in agony. The
police came to the conclusion that all these people had been
poisoned by the same fetish doctor, but all the evidence
implicating him had been carefully concealed and he was
never apprehended. The rule of the fetish doctor is absolute, because in the eyes of the natives the powers he repre-
sents are absolute.

Sometimes the powers of the fetish doctor are borrowed
by the natives. A perfectly normal native will suddenly go
berserk. He disappears and is never heard from again until
his body is discovered in the forest wrapped in a leopard
skin, with leopards' claws fastened to his hands and feet.
Suddenly, inexplicably, he has become a human leopard, and
must kill as leopards do. Or it may happen that he is forced
to become a human leopard against his will. One day he joins
a small group of men and drinks with them out of a human
skull filled with juices, then he is told that the juices were
mingled with the blood of a victim of a human leopard. Now
that he has drunk the potion, he cannot turn back. He must
join the leopard men, wear leopard clothes and learn how
to kill by striking with his claws at the carotid artery. In
addition he must provide a victim, preferably a young girl,
and lead her to a place where the leopard men can safely
attack her. Henceforward he belongs body and soul to the
leopard men, loses all contact with normal human society
and is at the mercy of the whims of the leopard men. Shortly
before Schweitzer's second journey to Africa, ninety natives
were arrested in the Ogowe region and charged with being

leopard men. They were imprisoned, and an attempt was made to extract confessions from them. None confessed. Somehow they obtained poisons. One day the prison officials discovered that all the imprisoned leopard men were dead; they had poisoned one another.

The natives of the Ogowe were at the mercy of superstition. After childbirth, the faces of mother and child were painted white to scare the devils away. They believed that all illness was produced by magic, and when they enter a hospital, they often brought with them someone they suspect of having produced the illness. He came under compulsion, and was sometimes killed if the patient was not cured. Always in the depths of the consciousness of the natives was the knowledge of magic powers, to sustain and fortify them. They were a sick people. For them magic was a way of life, a way to make life endurable. Modern man, turned outward, has lost the sense of his beginnings and his purpose on earth. The African, turned inward, finds it in the magic and symbolism of the witch doctors. Schweitzer learned early that when the white man destroys and discredits the African way of life, he is in danger of destroying the African's whole reason of existence. Only with the greatest gentleness and tact can the African be led into the strange pathways of modern civilization.

The Africans of the Ogowe are not entirely primitive. These remnants of eight powerful tribes possessed, and still possess, a culture of astonishing complexity. Their languages are rich and intricate, they have immense collections of songs and legends handed down from their ancestors, and they are excellent sculptors in ivory. Their textile designs are full of life and they are magnificent dancers and musicians.

Among these people, at Lambaréné, once ruled by the Sun King, Albert Schweitzer built a hospital. There are other hospitals in the Gabon Territory, many of them better equipped, and provided with better facilities for treatment and research, but the world has chosen to believe that the experiment of the Alsatian doctor is far more important than the official hospitals provided by the French colonial government. The world, as usual, is right. The hospital at Lambaréné became a legend because it satisfied the human needs of the Africans and represented the path that colonialism might have followed to success. There, if anywhere, was that spiritual and cultural arm which could have brought peace between the white man and the black man. In the West portentous importance was credited to the hospital at Lambaréné, because men dimly recognized its significance. Some who went there and saw how small a hospital it was wondered how the legend had arisen. Yet the legend remains. Like Guernica, Warsaw, Lidice it is a place written on the map of the spirit. There after long turmoil the power of light overcame the power of darkness. With a thousand more Lambarénés there might have been no revolt of Africa against the West.

Today at the age of 83 Schweitzer still rules the hospital he founded in 1913. A big, heavy, gruff man, wearing old-fashioned steel spectacles, with a thick mane of white hair, gentle, irascible, sometimes absurd, he behaves like a courtly patriarch. He looks like an aged planter from the Deep South and he wears his immense learning lightly. Because he belongs to the nineteenth century—he was born four years after the death of Livingstone—he seems to have stepped out of his own time. He is a mass of contradictions. He despises conventions and behaves conventionally. He detests governments and has said bitter things about established churches, but governments seek to honor him and the established churches are calling him "the greatest living Christian." He rules the hospital with the heavy hand of an autocrat and cries out continually against the "abysmal laziness of the African native" and insists upon segregating the white men and the black, but these things, culpable in any other man, are made tolerable by his essential good humor, his humanity and the fierce intellectual vigor with which he surveys the world's problems.

He is closer to the Promethean Faust than to the grave and simple-minded humanitarian. His earliest and most enduring passion was the study of the Last Days when the world shall be enveloped in flame and after a time of tribulation the Last Judgement shall be visited on the people of the earth. He thought continually in terms of ultimates. Theologian, musician, philosopher, the author of a classic study of Bach and a theological treatise which revolutionized religious thought in England and a philosophical work on the decay of the civilization we live in, he is not a man to be regarded lightly or to be cherished for his humanitarian impulses alone. He is usually portrayed as a gentle doctor who abandoned a succession of successful careers in Europe to live out the remainder of his life in an attempt to bring civilization to the natives of Equatorial Africa, but the portrait is only half true. Lightning flashes from his eyes. The motives that led him to Africa were fierce and compelling ones, and he never abandoned the three careers he had chosen before departing for Africa. Those who worship him—and they are many—are inclined to forget his intransigence, his ferocious self-dedication and the warfare in his soul, just as they are inclined to forget that he suffers from the sin of pride. It would be easy to draw up a list of his faults, but the list would be meaningless. In the end his greatest virtue was that he went to the heart of the problem of Africa long before men thought there was any problem at all. He knew very little about Africa, but he knew Lambaréné and this was enough.

Today, with Africa in turmoil, it becomes all the more necessary to understand why Schweitzer went to Africa and what he did there. There he stands, in an open white shirt and tattered mud-stained trousers and an eternal sun-helmet on his head, an old man in an ancient land—the symbol of the Africa that might have been, before the terrorists emerged with their guns.

~~~ 2 ~~~

A Fantastic Childhood

WHERE THE VOSGES MOUN-
tains dip towards the Rhine, among vineyards and ruined
castles set on the hills, on the edge of Alsace, in a country
which is neither France nor Germany but an embattled
borderland where for nearly fifteen hundred years the two
countries have faced each other, Albert Schweitzer was
born. "I am a tall pine tree of the Vosges," he said once,
meaning that his roots lay deep among those hills with their
rugged peaks and gently sloping valleys. He came from a
rich land, rooted in the past, fertilized by wars, and strangely
cut off from the present. A traveler in the remote towns of
Alsace feels that history has passed him by, forgetting that
in mediaeval times a good deal of history sprang from
there.

Schweitzer himself has never been able to forget his Alsatian heritage. In him German pride and French grace are
inextricably woven. In the mysterious way of Alsatians he
was able to absorb the best of both cultures and somehow
maintain an equilibrium between them. To the very end he
was to remain a man of the borderland, fiercely attached to

28

his independence. From the rugged hills of Alsace he drew his strength, and from the quiet valleys he drew his peace.

He was born on January 14, 1875, in the Protestant manse at Kaysersberg. Once Kaysersberg, which stands where the White River flows between dark hills, was the capital of Alsace, but in those days it was hardly more than a village living on its memories of imperial splendor, with a great crumbling castle looking down on the ruined walls and ancient stone fountains. Where a hundred thousand people once lived, there were now barely three thousand. Where Emperors and Chancellors had met, there was now only a handful of winegrowers and cotton spinners eking out a bare living. People remembered Kaysersberg because it was built by the Emperor Frederick II, *Stupor Mundi*, and because it was the birthplace of Johann Geyler von Kaysersberg, the great Catholic preacher of the Reformation, a man of powerful beliefs which he expressed with vigor and a classic sense of vituperation. In later years it pleased Schweitzer to remember two things about his birthplace: he was glad to be born in the same town as Johann Geyler, and in a year when the people of Kaysersberg celebrated a good vintage.

When he was born, his father had already accepted a call to serve in the village of Günsbach, some fifteen miles away in the valley of Münster. History, which weighed heavily on Kaysersberg, had left Günsbach untouched. It was a small village bedded between vineyards which are gently terraced along the rolling hillsides. The village roads were bordered with cherry trees, and there were plum trees

scattered about the slopes, while the crests of all the neighboring hills were thickly covered with beech and pine forests.
It was almost no village at all—a scattering of trim houses
on the river-bank, and the vineyards and forests crowding
near. There was a schoolhouse, a bakery, a butcher's shop,
a church perched on the slope of a hill with a tall steeple
and a stork's nest, to which the storks returned every year.
Wolves prowled the valley; goats and cows pastured on the
slopes. It is so small a village that you can pass it even today
without noticing it is there.

Shortly after his birth Albert Schweitzer nearly died. For
weeks his life hung in the balance. He was an ugly yellow
child with enormous grey-blue eyes, constantly suffering
from fevers which no doctors could cure. Six months after
his birth the baby was decked out in a white frock with
colored ribbons to attend his father's official installation at
the church. The baby looked close to death, and the villagers said fearfully in their Alsatian dialect: "*Das Bueble
isch die erschte Beerdigung wo der neue Pfarrer halte wird.*"
"The baby is going to be the new pastor's first funeral." His
mother heard the words and fled back to the bedroom of the
manse, her eyes red with tears. It was months later before
the baby was out of danger. He was saved by being made to
drink vast quantities of milk from neighbor Leopold's
cow.

As the boy grew up, his life revolved around the manse
and the small church on the hillside, where Catholic and
Protestant pastors took turns to guide their flocks. Every
Sunday at eight in the morning the bells rang to summon
the Catholic worshippers to Mass. Two hours later the bells

summoned the Protestants to Communion. Then Pastor Schweitzer would lead the service from below the high pulpit, speaking in German. At home he spoke in the Alsatian dialect and sometimes French, the language in which the Schweitzer family exchanged letters. From the beginning Albert was trilingual and sharply aware of the penalties which accompany a knowledge of too many languages.

The sick baby grew into a strong child. A photograph taken at the age of eight shows him in a velvet coat, a white collar and a flowing silk necktie, with a delicate feminine face, a stubby nose, a firm rounded chin and bright, inquiring eyes.

It was a strange childhood, and the ghosts were everywhere: the ghosts of the past, and the ghosts which sprang unbidden in the boy's feverish imagination as he looked out in indignation upon a world of poverty, a world where there was not enough food for the children of the manse, and his mother's eyes were too often red with weeping. The house was damp; food was cooked in vegetable oil, not in butter; the boy sometimes had to wear a thin summer suit through the long cold Alsace winters. For years poverty dogged them, made them often irritable. There were flares of temper. The weight of the misery fell on Albert's mother, who had somehow to provide food and sustenance for a large family on a pastor's tiny stipend. She did her best, provided her children with the two large bowls of gruel every day which gave them the strength to grow hard and lean, and overwhelmed them with her love.

Her health was good, but Pastor Schweitzer suffered from rheumatism and a stomach ailment and seems to have been curiously distant, a man seen rarely, forever scratching out sermons in his uncomfortable cluttered study, where the smell of damp musty books was overpowering: a man who would sometimes emerge vividly from the study in a tantrum, to box the ears of one of his sons: remembered most for his grace and dignity when he preached on Sundays in the nave of the little church at Günsbach, and then he seemed no longer like a father so much as a Father of the Church, a man impossibly learned, possessed of an uncommon gentleness and as though withdrawn from the world.

The boy reverenced his father, but he was closer to his mother, and perhaps he was closest of all to his mother's half-brother, the mysterious Uncle Albert from whom he derived his name, a ghostly figure, for Uncle Albert died three years before Albert was born, but his gentle and dominating influence survived him. "I was haunted by this man," Albert wrote later. "The thought came to me that in some way I would assume myself the responsibility for continuing the existence of a man who was so much loved by my mother." So, from his very earliest years and throughout his life, there was to be the continual celebration of a man never seen and whose image could only be guessed at. Albert Schweitzer, hero of Africa, was modelled on the obscure pastor, Albert Schillinger, hero of Strasbourg.

We know very little about Albert Schillinger, but we know enough to understand why he was worth imitating and why a boy should desire in some mysterious way to prolong the life of a dead uncle. Albert Schillinger was a saint, one of those small, quixotic and unpredictably generous men who are occasionally thrown into positions of prominence in the evangelical movement. He was pastor of the church of St. Nicholas in Strasbourg when the Franco-Prussian war broke out in 1870. Shortly after the first engagement between French and German troops at Wissembourg, the Germans trained their guns on Strasbourg. Pastor Schillinger slipped out of the city and made his way to Paris, hoping to return with medical supplies before the city was completely invested. In Paris there were delays. All available medical supplies had been sent to the French armies on the field. Bandages and medicaments were in short supply. The pastor went from one office to another, nearly always rebuffed. He pleaded for Strasbourg, told everyone who would listen about the unpreparedness of the city hospitals, of the dreadful effects of the coming bombardment on the civilian population if no medicines were sent through, and of how it was intolerable that Strasbourg should receive no mercy from the capital.

When at last he received a small stock of medicines, drugs and bandages, Strasbourg was already being heavily bombarded. Pastor Schillinger hurried back. When he reached the German lines he was captured and brought before General von Werder, the commander of the investing army. The general, who had no desire to continue the senseless bombardment—the decision had been made by von Moltke, the Chief of Staff—allowed the supplies to go through the lines and kept the pastor prisoner. Strasbourg was in flames. Thousands were dying. From his place of imprisonment the pastor could hear the shells pounding into the city, and he was tormented by the thought that his flock must have believed he deliberately refused to share their sufferings. It was the first example of the new barbarism: that terrible and costly destruction of a city at the orders of a German. The agonies of Strasbourg in the last days of August, 1870, are forgotten now, but at the time they filled the world with horror; and Pastor Schillinger, from the dubious safety of his prison, watched in terror as a defenceless people reeled under the shells of the guns standing wheel to wheel around the city. He was grief-stricken and convinced of his own guilt. He told himself it was his fault that not enough medicines had gone through. He should have shared the sufferings of the people of Strasbourg and died with them.

At last the siege came to an end, the people emerged from the smoking ruins, and the pastor was allowed to enter the city. The congregation of St. Nicholas greeted him with open arms, but he was never able to free himself completely from an overriding sense of guilt. There was a shortage of milk. Pastor Schillinger took care that his own share was given to old women and children. In the summer of 1872, exactly two years after the siege of Strasbourg, the saintly pastor dropped dead suddenly while talking to some friends. His heart, never strong, had cracked at last under the weight of grief and excitement.

The ghost of Pastor Schillinger was to pursue Albert Schweitzer throughout his life. Where the pastor had failed, Albert Schweitzer was determined to succeed; where the pastor had shown heroism, Schweitzer was to show the same. Instead of Strasbourg relentlessly ringed by German guns, starving for medicines, there was to be a quiet river in Africa, but this river was to be regarded as a stronghold and the people living on its banks were starving for medicines. And just as Pastor Schillinger in his extremity turned his face to Paris and there cajoled and coaxed and wheedled medical supplies from the protesting authorities, so in Africa Albert Schweitzer did the same. He modeled himself on his uncle, conjured his uncle's image from the grave, and in the end he was to fulfill the promise he had made to his mother: he continued the existence of the man his mother had loved so greatly.

But Pastor Schillinger was only one of many ghosts, even if he was the most important of them all. There was the ghost of Grandfather Schillinger, a courtly, tempestuous man, an expert organist with a passion for building organs and inspecting them—once, hearing of a new organ in Lucerne, Switzerland, he made a journey for no other purpose than to try it out. Grandfather Schillinger was pastor of the town of Mühlbach in the Münstertal, higher up the valley. His manners belonged to the eighteenth century. He could be sharply imperious and quick-tempered when he felt he was not receiving the respect he deserved, but he could also be wryly humorous. He had a pleasant habit of setting up his telescope outside his house on starlit nights and inviting passersby to gaze at the heavens. Schweitzer believes he inherited his terrible temper from his maternal grandfather. From his father he inherited his timidity and the habit of losing himself in dreams.

Timidity plagued him. In later years he came to wonder whether in all Günsbach there was a child as timid as himself. It was not the timidity which comes from fear so much as a natural self-absorption, and a greater faith in the validity of the world of the imagination than that of the world he saw around him. He was given to introspection, sudden fits of weeping, inexplicable bursts of laughter—one of his teachers gave him for this reason the name of Isaac, which means "laughter" in Hebrew. He would be haunted for weeks by the sight of an old limping horse. To see someone in pain drove him to the edge of madness. Moody and reserved, his passionate temper at war with his natural caution, he learned to live in the imagination. His first memory was of seeing the devil.

He was three years old when he met the devil face to face. Afterwards he remembered every detail of the devil's appearance, as he remembered the touch of a servant girl's cotton gloves on his lips when he yawned in church. The devil appeared on Sunday close to the organ, but only when the organ was being played, vanishing when his father mounted the pulpit. After the prayers, the devil appeared again, a great shaggy face, roving eyes, very stern and commanding. Whenever the organ was playing and the congregation singing, there was the devil; whenever his father was praying or delivering a sermon, the devil vanished. The boy had his own simple explanation. "The devil is gazing down at the people in the church," he told himself, "but as soon as my father speaks the Word of God, the devil makes himself scarce!" He was fascinated by the appearance of the devil and looked forward, in fear and trembling, to seeing that monstrous and shaggy face every Sunday. It was some years before he learned that the devil was only the head of bearded Father Iltis, the organist, reflected in a mirror above the organ as he sat at the manuals.

There were other and more human devils. There was old

Jaegle, the sacristan and grave-digger, a fierce little peasant with a gift for pure malevolence. Every Sunday morning he came early to the manse, carefully wiped his feet on the doormat and rang the bell. Albert was sent to answer the door and give Jaegle the numbers of the hymns; later the sacristan would insert the numbers on a board and give the information to Father Iltis. Because Albert had a bulging forehead, Jaegle would rub his knotted hands over it and declare: "Well, the horns are growing, eh?" For the boy it was unremitting torture. He was continually running his fingers over the bulges on his forehead, and he was sure the horns were growing there. He was wholly in Jaegle's power, and felt like a fascinated rabbit in the stare of a snake. Every Sunday there was this terrible hurdle. For a year the boy suffered in secret. At last he went to his father, confessed his fears, and learned that Moses was the only man who had ever lived who wore horns. Then he lost his fears.

But old Jaegle knew his victim well, knew exactly how to impose on the boy's timidity. An old soldier, he had fought in the French Army in the Crimean War. Now that Alsace had become part of Germany following the Franco-Prussian War, it amused the old man to remember that in Prussia everyone has to be a soldier, and soldiers of course wear iron clothes. "Look out," he would say. "Soon you will have to go up the street to the blacksmith and get fitted for your iron clothes." The boy obeyed. He was forever standing outside the blacksmith's shop and waiting for the moment when the first soldiers would come to demand their armor, as in the Middle Ages. This time the boy confessed his fears to his mother, who told him that armor had been abandoned for some years: when the time came for the boy to be drafted into the German Army, he would wear clothes made out of cloth like the rest. Once again old Jaegle had been proved wrong.

Yet Jaegle was not so very far wrong. The lonely, moody boy growing up in the manse at Günsbach had one foot in the Middle Ages. In the evenings before going to bed he listened to his mother reading the stories of Sir Walter Scott. These were her favorite reading, and her greatest desire was to travel to Scotland and walk on the earth once trodden by Rob Roy. She filled him with stories of knights in armor and of prodigious battles in mountain glens, and then when he walked along the winding roads which stretch from Günsbach over the hills, he would imagine himself in a mysterious Scotland of legend. He loved the hills. He spoke of them as "my protectors"; they sheltered and companioned him on his long lonely walks, and they seemed alive. For him the earth breathed, and the forests and vineyards clothed the living form of the earth, and every place was sacred. One place was more sacred than the rest—the Rochers de Kanzenrain, the sharp outcrops overlooking the vineyards above Günsbach. These rocks were his secret hidingplace. There he would disappear on long, lonely, meditative journeys, and gaze up the valley towards Münster and the heights of the Hoheneck, the highest of all the Vosges mountains, in the distance. From here, too, he could see the romantic ruined castle called the Schwarzenburg, perched on a hilltop beyond the river, once belonging to the Count von Hartmann whose knights ruled this river valley as their private preserve. In summer blue mists filled the valley in the late afternoons. Far away he could see the blue-smocked women in the vineyards. He was happiest when he was alone, lying on the sun-warmed rock, dreaming his life away.

Two moods ruled him—an extraordinary, almost pagan, feeling for nature, and a piercing sensitivity to pain. In later years he could never remember a time when he was not brutally aware of pain, just as he could never remember a time when he knew the normal *joie de vivre* of youth. Pain was the enemy, ruthless, immutable, eternally mocking. It was something that happened usually in the village, not in the forests and the uplands. Pain was a limping horse in the street or an old freckled grey-bearded Jew who came wandering into Günsbach with a donkey cart, while the village boys ran after him, jeering and screaming. Pain was a dog rolling over and howling in the snow after the young Schweitzer had lashed out with a whip and caught it across the eyes. True, the dog was known to be vicious and had come bounding across the street, leaping straight at a horse's head. True, the horse would have suffered pain if the dog had got its teeth into it, and the pain suffered by the dog was perhaps no greater than the pain that would have been suffered by the horse. But that there should be pain in the world at all remained the mystery, perhaps the greatest of all mysteries. And so he would sometimes cry himself to sleep, asking himself why so many living creatures had to suffer pain. It seemed to him that all living creatures were dedicated to pain. In the evenings, after praying with his mother, he would add his own silent prayer for all living creatures: "Dear God, protect and bless all things that breathe, guard them from all evil and let them sleep in peace."

Sometimes the fact of pain shocked him into violent and repeated resolves to so order his life that he would inflict no pain on anything that lived and breathed. Twice in his life he went fishing. The second time he was so appalled by the torments of the worms wriggling on the hook and by the torn mouths of fishes that he resolved never to go fishing again, and went about begging the village boys to give up the sport. Another time, when he was seven or eight, he went out bird-hunting with a friend. The sun was shining. The birds were singing on the trees. Like his friend he was armed with a catapult. At the moment when young Schweitzer stooped to gather a stone to insert in the catapult, the Easter bells rang out. It was like a sign from Heaven. He began to shout and wave his arms, shooing the bird away, then he fled home. He had discovered the commandment which was to weigh increasingly on him over the years: "Thou shalt not kill!"

In those early years he showed no signs of brilliance. He disliked the village school and was an unwilling pupil. He learned to read and write with immense difficulty. He was the parson's son, "a sprig of the gentry," and aware of the difference of class which separated him from the village boys. He wanted to conform, to be like them, to be accepted by them. The village boys went about in clogs, wearing leather boots only on Sundays; he decided stubbornly he would do the same. They wore fingerless mittens; he refused to wear the gloves his father ordered him to wear. None of the village boys possessed heavy winter overcoats. When his father cut down an overcoat to his size, the boy refused to wear it—one whole winter was made miserable by these continual refusals. He was boxed on the ears and beaten with a stick. It made no difference. He had his mother's passionate temper, her complete inability to compromise with her convictions. He would not wear a sailor cap; he must wear the brown cap which can be pulled down over the ears; then he would look like one of the village boys. But he did not look like them. They taunted him continually with the words which bit deep into his soul: "Here comes the parson's son!" They never guessed what torments he went through in his ceaseless struggle to be regarded as one of them.

A quiet and dreamy schoolboy, with almost no talent for school-work, he was already enjoying music. In the manse there was an old square piano which had once belonged to his grandfather Schillinger. The boy was five years old when he practiced his first scales under his father's tutelage. His father had little gift for playing from sheet music. He improvised, played variations on themes, reproduced hymn tunes to his accompaniment. He was not a particularly good teacher, and the boy was not a particularly good pupil. He was clumsy and held his fingers awkwardly, but at least he used both hands, unlike the teacher of singing in the village school who pecked out hymn tunes with one finger. One day the boy asked the teacher why she did not play the music with the harmony. The truth was that she had no knowledge of harmony. The boy sat down at the piano and played with the proper harmony, delighting the teacher "who began to look at me in a new and unusual way." For himself, he was alarmed. He had attracted attention. He was not conforming. And he did not play for her again.

Conformity was the mask he wore, but sometimes his rebellious spirit broke through. Sometimes he could not prevent himself from crying out against the errors of his betters. He was beginning to be one of those terrible children who know all the answers. He was forever asking his father insoluble questions. When he was eight his father gave him a New Testament. He read it eagerly. The harassed pastor would find himself staring into the bright eyes of his son and listening to conundrums: "What did Mary and Joseph do with the gold and frankincense and myrrh they received from the Three Wise Men from the East? Why were the parents of Jesus so poor when so much treasure had been heaped upon them? And what happened to the Three Wise Men afterwards and to the shepherds of Bethlehem—why is nothing more said about them?" The boy was particularly puzzled by the fate of the shepherds, for good reason. Asked once what he was going to be when he grew up, he answered that he wanted to be a shepherd or a swineherd. He would pass his life in the foothills, with nature and animals as his companions. He was nearly fifteen before it occurred to him that he might spend his life with music and theology as his companions.

So the years passed in the village school. He learned to read and write; he learned to compromise a little; he liked the village boys with their wooden clogs and darned woollen stockings, their brown caps and the slates they carried eternally under their arms; he grew accustomed to being "a sprig of the gentry." But his real life was with his family.

There were two tyrants in the house—his father, and the maidservant whose duty was to see that he was properly washed and dressed before he went to school. The maid had her own ideas about conformity. Albert had unruly hair. To his horror, it had to be slicked down every morning with the help of a yellow stick of brilliantine, which she rubbed into his scalp. Then she would brush the hair vigorously and painfully, then comb it, then contrive a neat parting, all the while murmuring ominously: "There's a lot in the way the hair grows . . . If you're a mess outside, you're a mess inside as well." She had an endless repertoire of insults which she directed against his hair. It was no use. An hour later the hair, so carefully smeared with perfumed brilliantine, was as unruly as before, and there was no sign of the parting she had brought into being with so much patience and art.

There were many happy interludes. There were those rare days when his father descended from his high eminence, no longer a stranger enshrined in his book-cluttered study. There was the day when a man on a bicycle came to the village inn. The children were playing in the schoolyard when the news arrived. They had never seen a bicycle before. They went screaming into the street to see the prodigy who wore knickerbockers and was solemnly drinking a glass of wine in the inn. Breathless, they waited for him to emerge, and they almost died with laughing when he swung his leg over the wheel and rode off. It was one of those bicycles which consisted of one small wheel and one immense wheel, with a little padded seat on top.

In summer Italian peasant women came flocking down

the Münster valley with baskets filled with fowl, and it
amused him to watch his mother buying them and then
setting the foreign fowl down on the barnyard floor. At first
the Italian fowl walked very shyly and humbly, uncertain
of themselves. In time, of course, they behaved as proudly
and pompously as the fowl of Alsace. To the boy who still
felt himself a stranger in the world, there were lessons to be
learned even from hens and chicks.

Best of all, there was music. Though he played artlessly,
music tore at his soul. One day in the village school, while
he was waiting outside a classroom, he heard the children
singing a two-part harmony:

In the mill by the stream where I was sunk in silent thought,
O beautiful forest, who planted you there?

The words, and the splendor of the harmonized voices, were
like a shock on exposed nerves. He had never heard anything so beautiful. He almost fainted from excess of pleasure
over the voluptuous beauty of the duet, sung by boys only
a little older than himself. A little while later he received
the same pleasurable shock when he heard brass instruments
playing in harmony. These unexpected discoveries in harmony made him more than ever determined to practice
religiously on the square piano. He made quick strides. At
seven he was composing his own hymns. At eight, when his
feet could scarcely reach the pedals, he played on the organ
in the Günsbach church, sometimes substituting for Father
Iltis. At nine he even dared to play in Grandfather Schillinger's old church at Mühlbach on a glorious instrument built
by Pastor Schillinger himself under the direction of a famous

organ builder called Stier. Now at last he was free of second-rate instruments; he had heard the sounds a great organ can give, and he was never to forget them.

The year he was nine, the boy was sent off to school in Münster, two miles down the valley. Here in the seventh century the Benedictine monks had established themselves and built the *Monasterium Sancti Gregorii,* from which Münster derives its name. Nothing remained of the Benedictine Abbey except an old ruined tower on top of the Monchsberg. It was a small manufacturing town, which had long ago forgotten its proud mediaeval past when it was a free city of the German Empire. Albert spent a year at the school. He walked there every morning and walked back every evening, nearly always alone, cherishing his loneliness. For the first time he was moved to write poetry. The poems were terrible; so were the drawings he made of the Schwarzenburg Castle. He decided he had talent neither for poetry nor drawing, and began to take a lively interest in history. He went to the *Realschule,* a secondary school where no Greek was taught and education tended away from the age-long supremacy of the classics. Religious instruction was given by Pastor Schaffler, who was given to oratorical improvisations on Bible stories, telling them with such effect that the boys sometimes found themselves weeping uncontrollably. Pastor Schaffler wept easily. The story of how Joseph revealed himself to his brethren was particularly effective. It was Pastor Schaffler who gave Albert the nickname of "Isaac," because he laughed so often and so nervously, possessing no natural gaiety. Shy, reserved, usually speaking only when spoken to, though sometimes he would launch out in violent dinner-table disputations, the boy was far more interested in his lonely walks to school than in anything he learned there.

That year was famous for the good wine which came from the vineyards in the Münster valley, but for Albert it was a year of constant introspection. He rejoiced in his loneliness. He worked diligently—at Latin, at mathematics, at the natural sciences. He disliked them all. He was feeling his way, more than ever convinced that he would be happiest as a swineherd or a shepherd. Once in the summer, standing on the edge of a pine forest, he saw a royal stag lifting his antlers before darting away: the memory of that silent confrontation was to haunt him forever.

About this time he discovered abstractions. He was about four when he saw the devil. He was about eight when he came face to face with Evil for the first time. It was during the summer holiday when he was staying with his godmother. Two maid-servants were ordered to take the boy for a short walk and never to lose sight of him. The maid-servants went off to a country-fair, taking the boy with them. Soon they were all dancing a *contre-danse*, the two maids squeezing the boy between them while they attended to more interesting matters with their cavaliers. "You mustn't tell anyone you went to the fair," they told him afterwards. He promised not to tell, but he was shocked by the guilt he was so casually assuming. What would he do—what *could* he do—if his godmother asked him where he had been? Mercifully, she only asked him whether he had spent a happy afternoon. "Very happy," he answered, and shivered at the thought of the unspoken question.

On another day he was entrusted to the care of a boy a few months older than himself. His godmother told him he must not go near the river, and above all he must not go on one of the river boats. The two children found themselves on the shore, gazing enviously at the river boats piled high with vegetables sailing downstream. It was a time when Albert's ambitions was violently fluctuating. The desire to be a swineherd was temporarily abandoned, and he had decided to become a coachman, then a pastrycook. Now, quite suddenly, he decided to be a sailor. The two boys found a boat which was not properly tied up, and spent an enjoyable afternoon skimming along the river, surrounded by the beautiful vegetable boats. When they returned, they found the boat-owner waiting for them. Both boys were heavily punished, and Albert, already possessed of a stern protestant conscience, regarded his own guilty disobedience with horror. Once again Evil had entered the world as the result of disobedience to a higher power.

Disobedience, laziness, daydreaming, sudden violent arguments, nervous titters—the boy showed all the signs of developing into a ne'er-do-well with a talent for musical improvisation. The time had come to take his measure. In despair the old pastor called upon the help of a half-brother, Louis Schweitzer, director of the Mulhouse primary schools. Uncle Louis saw little hope for the boy, but offered to put him to school at the Gymnasium at Mulhouse and to supervise his education. The offer, which included free board, was gratefully accepted, and Albert was packed off on a train, to spend the next eight years with his uncle.

The fantastic childhood was not yet over. There was

something of a child in Albert Schweitzer during all the years he spent at the Gymnasium—a child's directness, a child's sudden devotions. He saw the dreary industrial town through the eyes of a boy who longed for the countryside, longing especially for his solitary walks or those ceremonial walks shared by the whole family every Sunday, a stroll down the valley followed by a climb through the woods and vineyards, with his father always at the head of the procession. He longed, too, for the little church in Günsbach and the sight of his father in black gown and Geneva bands, wearing the toque which had been handed down by his father before him. Life in the Münster valley was primitive, earthy, as sacramental as the lives of the ancient Israelites. Now for the first time the boy was confronted with a roaring city.

~~~ 3 ~~~
A Hind in the City

IN THEIR COLD, CLUTTERED, uncomfortable apartment inside the school building, Uncle Louis and Aunt Sophie lived lives of classic boredom. They were childless. They were *bourgeois*. They were very German. They were not happy to have Albert in their midst, and they accepted their new responsibility only out of a sense of outraged family duty.

Uncle Louis was a disciplinarian, a short fat man devoted to the task of superintending the schools, with simple tastes and a great respect for official rules and regulations. Like his wife, he lived by the clock. On most subjects he possessed firm and unalterable opinions, and he had almost no vices. He was stern, uncompromising and full of genuine religious feeling. He half-detested schoolchildren and he tolerated their inadequacies only with the greatest distaste.

Aunt Sophie was made of sterner metal. Tight-lipped, grimly concerned with the proprieties, she superintended the household with a firm hand. She had timed her day to the last minute—so many hours for housework, so many hours for eating, so many hours for reading romantic novels.

Exactly half an hour before supper she took up a book—she
passionately enjoyed Daudet and Victor Hugo and had a
fondness for books "written in a good style"—and when the
supper plates had been cleared away, she would read for
exactly two hours again. At half past ten, even if she was
in the middle of a sentence, she would close her book and
announce that it was time for bed. She regarded punctuality
and obedience as the supreme virtues. She taught Albert to
be attentive to his elders, to keep his mouth shut, to be clean
at all times and to bear the injustices of fate with a Christian
demeanor, with the result that when he escaped from her
tutelage, he threw overboard all her crisply enunciated precepts, refused to obey the clock, worked whenever he
wanted to, and became a bohemian. She disliked his passion for reading the newspapers, and told him so. She suspected—rightly—that he enjoyed reading accounts of murder trials, and so she forbade him to read the newspapers
altogether. One day during supper, when he insisted tear-
fully that he *had* to read the newspapers otherwise he would
not know what was happening in the world, Uncle Louis
said: "We'll soon see whether this young idiot really reads
the political pages," and forced Albert to submit to a prolonged examination. Who were the members of the last
three French cabinets? Name all the ruling princes of the
Balkans and all the Prime Ministers of the Balkan countries.
Young Albert came through the examination with flying
colors, and when the baked potatoes and salad were cleared
away, he was told he had shown exemplary understanding
of current political problems. He would therefore be allowed
to read newspapers for fifteen minutes before supper and

again for a brief while after he had finished his homework.

The shadow of Aunt Sophie with her provincial ways,
her little austerities and her harsh and constantly repeated
moral precepts fell heavily on his school years at Mulhouse.
"She was all for hardening me," he wrote later. "She believed that reserve was the essence of good breeding and
every kind of forwardness was a crime." He learned to hate
her stiffness and reserve, and to detest those who trample on
the natural forwardness of youth. Even her kindnesses were
cold. One day in March, when the last snows were melting
on the hills, he was sitting over his homework, gazing at
the wooded hills through the window, lost in dreams. It was
four o'clock in the afternoon, the time when coffee was
served. Aunt Sophie was hovering over her ironing board.
She must have seen the dreadful look of longing on his face,
for suddenly she stopped ironing and said: "Let's go out and
have a walk." He was utterly astonished. They went out
together, crossed the canal where the ice was still floating,
and climbed Stag Hill, and it was dark when they returned,
having exchanged no more than a few polite phrases. It was
all very odd. Sometimes he would find himself wondering
at her sudden change of heart, but she never invited him to
walk with her again.

The school, too, was cold. In winter there was almost no
heating. The pupils shivered, and went mechanically
through their lessons. At first he hated the school as much
as he hated the clammy house where he lived. A day came
when Uncle Louis was compelled to send for Pastor
Schweitzer and report that his son showed no signs of prog-

ress: it would be better perhaps if the scholarship were
offered to a more deserving candidate. Albert was not
scolded. He was told he could have one more chance.
There must be no more daydreaming. Did he want to become a swineherd or a man of character, a scholar like his
grandfather? The short colloquy with his father determined the matter. By a sheer act of will Albert decided to
throw himself into his studies with the same enthusiasm that
he had shown for the newspapers.

It was not always easy. Sometimes the fits of daydreaming returned. There was little to choose between the austerities of the school and the austerities of his uncle's house.
For a while austerity itself became the boy's passion. He
studied his teachers. There was Dr. Wehrmann, a harsh and
nervous pedagogue with a talent for crisp explanation and
a flair for exactness, who always prepared his lessons to the
last minute detail. Watching Dr. Wehrmann, the boy was
suddenly struck with the thought that "what has been begun
must be finished." The doctor was all steel, and it was pure
pleasure to watch the working of his rigorous, logical mind.
Rigor however did not make him happy. He went from one
job to another, and at some time during the First World
War, suffering from starvation and nervous exhaustion, he
killed himself.

The boy was an excellent student in history and the natural sciences, and was nearly hopeless in mathematics. He
was no good in literature, and took a particularly violent
dislike to Homer. The lessons in which lines of poetry were
explained by the professor he found hateful, silly and un-
nerving; it was much better to read poetry without the dubi-

ous aid of a professor. In science classes he was amused by
the formal textbook explanations of the nature of things—
they seemed so pitifully small in comparison with the gran-
deur he had observed in his lonely wanderings. He found it
impossible to believe in the simple textbook explanations of
wind, rain, snow, hail, thunder, lightning; and thinking of
these splendid manifestations of power and of the mysterious
flow of life in the heavens and on earth, he found himself
daydreaming again, lost in the miraculous. Though he fell
easily under the influence of his teachers, he kept the hard
core of himself untouched.

One man—and only one man—was able to break
through the boy's inmost reserve. This was the strange, trust-
ing, generous and infinitely patient genius, Eugen Münch,
the organist at the church of St. Stephen. With his thick
black beard and dark hair brushed back from an immense
square forehead, Münch dominated the musical life at Mulhouse. The boy took lessons from him. At first Münch found
no merit in him. "He is a thorn in my flesh!" Münch ex-
claimed, and meant it, and very nearly stopped giving Albert
lessons. "It's a waste of time making you feel, because you
have no feeling in you," he said on another occasion.

One day after he had murdered a Mozart sonata, Münch
gave him a passage from Mendelssohn's *Lieder ohne Worter*
to play, saying: "You don't deserve to have such beautiful
music given to you—you'll murder it as you have murdered
everything else!" The boy took the music home, determined
this time to prove himself. He studied the music for a week.
He carefully examined the proper fingering. He played the
piece until he knew it by heart, until every nuance was

familiar to him. When next time he played for Münch, the
demon of music had taken up its dwelling-place in his heart,
with such unexpected fire and passion that the teacher could
only gape and press the boy's shoulders. Soon he was allowed to play Bach and was told he could take his organ
lessons on the great organ in St. Stephen's church with its
three keyboards and thirty-two stops. He no longer cared
very deeply for his studies: he was becoming a musician.

Many people left their impress on Schweitzer's mind, but
it is possible that the most important were Albert Schillinger and Eugen Münch, who suffered from deafness and died
young, saying on his deathbed that he did not mind leaving
his children behind, because he knew they would be well
cared for, but he was appalled at the thought of leaving his
musical children, the choral singers, the members of the
Chant Sacré at St. Stephen's church, for no one else in
Mulhouse would be able to train them as he had done. And
at the very last moments of his life he consoled himself with
the thought that he would be an organist in heaven. A few
months after Münch's death Albert Schweitzer wrote in
French a little brochure intended for the family and friends
of the dead organist.

About the time when he was first taking piano lessons
from Münch, Schweitzer attended his first public concert,
given in the hall of the stock exchange in Mulhouse. It was
a gala occasion, with everyone in evening dress and young
Schweitzer in his best Sunday suit. The musician was Marie-
Joseph Erb, who is forgotten now, but in his day he was
regarded as a virtuoso player of the highest accomplishment.
Years later, when Schweitzer was an accomplished organist

of world-wide fame, he set down his memories of the first public concert he ever attended:

M. Erb sat down at the piano, played a prelude until there was complete silence, and then spiritedly launched an attack on the first number of the program. For the first time I realized what a *virtuoso* was. I was stunned to see his hands moving so swiftly across the keyboard. He knew it all by heart, never hesitated, never made a mistake. I was overwhelmed with astonishment. With my little knowledge of the piano, I attempted to understand how he contrived to produce these cascades of arpeggios, these explosions of shooting stars, all the while retaining clarity in the melody, achieving *pianissimi* in which no single notes were ever lost.

Those first piano pieces kept me in a state of bubbling excitement. Afterwards the artist rose, bowed to a wildly applauding audience, then vanished behind a door, only to reappear when the applause failed to die down, then he vanished, then appeared again, and once more vanished behind the door. At last there was silence. People were busy studying their programs. The women in the audience offered each other sweetmeats. And it seemed strange to me that these people in the audience, who had applauded so heartily, were no longer under his spell. They were chattering to each other as though nothing at all had taken place.

At last M. Erb returned, smiling and taking his place beside the *chanteuse*, a woman who wore her hair in curls like the curls of little girls at their first communion. She wore long white gloves. She placed an immense bouquet of flowers on a chair. She curtseyed, she opened wide the sheet music, her hands trembling a little, then she coughed slightly and glanced at the musician, making a slight sign with her head. At once the musician launched upon the first measures of the accompaniment. I was aware of the beauty of the singing, but I was still more aware of the accompanist, who was so superbly equipped to follow her singing, going faster or slower according to the tempo of her singing, as she went from *pianissimo* to *fortissimo* and returned from *fortissimo* to *pianissimo*. He was possessed of an incredible adaptability. His display of virtuosity took my breath away. For me it was a startling revelation of all the possibilities of the piano. As I walked home, I was like someone in a dream.

During the following days I labored over my scales, my finger exercises and the Czerny *études* with unparalleled ardor, even when they were thickly scattered with sharps and double sharps, which I had always previously detested.

In later days I heard the most celebrated piano *virtuosi*. None of them ever moved me so deeply as Marie-Joseph Erb, when I first set eyes on him as a young student at college.[1]

For Albert Schweitzer, Mulhouse was music, history and science, and mostly it was music. He told himself that music was the splendor around which his life would revolve. He was fifteen when Eugen Münch took him into the organ loft of St. Stephen's church and taught him the strict use of the pedals; within a year he was allowed to play the organ accompaniment of Brahms' *Requiem* while the robed choir sang. He had known the glory of playing a well-built organ before when he played on his grandfather's organ at Mühlbach, but the Mulhouse organ was even finer, though set in an ugly jerry-built church without a chancel and without any of the glittering decoration which made him so happy in the church at Günsbach. Here for the first time he was aware of the immense *power* possessed by a full-throated organ playing with a full orchestra and a choir of choristers. "Here at last," he wrote later, "I knew the special joy, so

[1] *Un Grand Musicien Francais: Marie-Joseph Erb. Strasbourg-Paris.* F. X. Le Roux & Cie, p. 83–84.

often tasted afterwards, of being at an organ from which
there came a welling flood of music mingling with the clam-
orous music of choir and orchestra."

Oddly, for one who was descended from generations of
Lutheran pastors, there was yet no sign of religious feeling.
He suffered like nearly all the students of his time from a
Romantic *Weltschmerz*: he was in love with nature, and
could be moved to tears by the chorales of Bach; he was
excited by religious paintings and could remember in vivid
detail long excerpts of the sermons spoken by his father in
the church in Günsbach on Sunday afternoons; but faith
escaped him. He had questioned some of the pronounce-
ments of the Bible when he was a boy. As a college student,
he came to believe that Christianity must submit to reason,
that it was valid only where it could be defended by reason.
He had a grave respect for old Pastor Wennagel, his instruc-
tor at the time of his confirmation, but the old pastor insisted
that reason was blind and that all reason must be silenced
before the mysteries of faith. Schweitzer rebelled. It seemed
to him that there was no limit to the power of reason, that
everything must bow to its ordinances, even the most exalted
religious concepts.

During confirmation classes, Schweitzer remained stubbornly silent, with no desire to cross swords with a venerable
pastor, who reported to Uncle Louis that the boy was possessed of a spirit of indifference. In fact, Schweitzer was
desperately aware of the sanctity of confirmation, and he
said later that he spent those weeks of preparation like
someone bathed in a spirit of holiness, not knowing where
to turn except to the face of God; and when on Palm Sun-

day the candidates for confirmation walked in procession from the vestry into the church, nothing was so wonderful as the moment when Eugen Münch began to play "Lift up your heads, O ye gates!" from Handel's *Messiah*. Then at last he saw that music received its greatest sanction when placed at the service of the solemn rites of the church.

It was the year of quickening—the year of his confirmation, the year when he became completely aware of his musical powers, the year when he began to see the whole of his life stretching before him. That year, too, in Günsbach, things were changing for the better. His father's health improved. The old manse, draughty and damp, overshadowed by other buildings, was exchanged for a large new dwelling house set in a sunny garden, and not long afterwards there was an improvement in the family fortunes when a distant relative died childless and left them a small fortune. Henceforward the manse rang with happiness, and between Albert and his father there was no longer a sense of strangeness. His childhood was bitter, but after the age of fourteen he complained only against his excessive happiness, which seemed in some way undeserved, and even unjust, so that he began to ask himself why he had been chosen for so great a grace. Confusedly, he saw that his present happiness and the intense awareness of pain which shadowed his childhood were somehow related. He could not tell how they were related. The two experiences melted into one another. But he knew even then that in some way he would have to reconcile the conflict. Against the enemy pain he would wage war, but on what battleground? He did not know then, and could not have guessed, that he would spend so many

exasperating years studying medicine, where the disciplines
are curiously at odds with the disciplines of music. He was
in good health, ruddy-cheeked, powerfully built, good at his
studies by dint of perseverance, already an extremely gifted
musician: no sickness or misery had touched him. There
were moments when he was tempted to regard himself as
"the lord of his own life," the pure romantic endowed with
such gifts that he had only to exploit them to his own advantage and find the world at his feet. But these moments
passed; and if the wings of pride fanned his forehead, they
left no trace. Sometimes he would look upon his own growing sense of responsibility as a small cloud above the horizon. He was still in his teens when he saw the cloud growing
until it covered the whole sky.

But in the early summer of 1893, when he was nineteen,
coming to the end of his long years at the Gymnasium, there
were more immediate problems to contend with. The final
examinations were on the way, and he was faced with the
problem of what to do next. He passed the examinations
satisfactorily, he was then faced with a *viva voce*. On such
occasions students wore starched collars, black ties and
frock coats. He possessed a frock coat which had been
handed down from his relatives, but he had to borrow the
trousers from his uncle, who was short and fat. Albert
Schweitzer was lean and tall. He wore the trousers, using
suspenders lengthened with string, but there was a gap between the top of the trousers and the waistcoat. When he
entered the hall where the *viva voces* were being given, even
the examiners burst out laughing. Only Professor Albrecht,
who was in charge of the *viva voce*, refused to see anything

funny in Schweitzer's appearance and asked tartly what the merriment was all about. Schweitzer had always detested Homer, particularly detesting the genealogies of the heroes and the long catalogues of ships. Almost inevitably it happened that Professor Albrecht's first question asked for a detailed account of how the ancient Greeks maneuvered their ships. Schweitzer did not know. None of the other students could answer the question. Professor Albrecht's temper flared up, and he denounced them for their "serious defects in culture." (Schweitzer was privately concerned with another aspect of the cultural defects of the Gymnasium —after nearly ten years of science, he had not been given a single lesson in geology or astronomy.) Finally, he was asked questions in history, his special study. What was the difference between the colonization methods of the ancient Greeks and the ancient Romans? The question made sense; he answered it well; and soon the terrible-tempered School Commissioner, sent down from Strasbourg, was gentle as a lamb. On Schweitzer's school-leaving certificate, otherwise innocuous, there was a commendatory inscription praising his knowledge of history. But if Professor Albrecht thought he had made a historian out of Schweitzer, he was wrong. He had already decided upon his course of study at the university: he had decided to become simultaneously a theologian, a philosopher, and a musical theorist.

The man was formed by the time he was fourteen, and most of the influences that went to form him have now been described. One other influence, which acted like a catalytic agent on the rest, has been left to the last. This was Colmar, an ancient city set amid orchards and green

wooded hills some twelve miles from Günsbach at the head
of the Münster valley. Colmar, though the capital of Alsace,
was a small city surrounded by a mediaeval wall, living on
its dreams of mediaeval magnificence. Once, in the year
1226, it had been declared a free town of the Empire by the
Emperor Frederick II. Two hundred and fifty years later
the people of Colmar refused admittance to Charles the
Bold. Wars had swept the Swedes and the French up to the
gates of the city. With its gabled roofs and brightly painted
houses, the inevitable ruined castle perched on the hill
above, it seemed to have slipped away from the nineteenth
century altogether.

Nearly every summer Schweitzer spent part of his holidays at Colmar as the guest of his favorite godmother, Mme.
Julie Fellner-Barth. He took piano lessons from her daughter, who complained that he held his fingers awkwardly and
was always forgetting his lessons. Market-day in Colmar
fell on Thursday, and it was the practice on Thursdays to
invite visitors to lunch and then take them on a tour of the
town, ending up with the museum. On that day entrance to
the museum was free. Once the museum had been a Domin-
ican monastery, now it was a treasure-house of paintings
and the best works of Martin Schongauer and Grünewald
hung on its walls. Here in a dark corner stood the greatest
of Grünewald's paintings—the Isenheimer Altar.

When Schweitzer visited Paris and wandered through the
Louvre, it seemed to him that the treasures of the Colmar
Museum were far superior to anything he found in Paris.
There was nothing in the Louvre to compare with some of
the paintings of Schongauer or the great altarpiece, which

fascinated him with its sombre violence. The central figure
in the altarpiece is Christ crucified, in agony, blood dripping
from the crown of thorns, mouth open as he sobs out his last
breath, the flesh already green. Here with astonishing
brilliance was depicted the element of pain, which Schweitzer
feared and detested ever since he could remember. The
Virgin looks on. Her face is frozen with horror, and she has
fallen into the arms of the Beloved Disciple. Schweitzer had
good reason to remember the Beloved Disciple, who is represented as a typical German student of the period, with
limp unruly straw-colored hair. It occurred to Schweitzer
that if the Beloved Disciple did not comb his hair, there was
no reason for him to apologise for his own untidiness, and
he remembered the heavy insults of the maid who had
attempted so unsuccessfully to transform him with the help
of a stick of yellow brilliantine. It consoled him to have
something in common with St. John. He reasoned that if
St. John could go about with uncombed hair, even to being
present at the Crucifixion with all those marks of his unruly
character, then the maid was wrong in believing that there
was any relation between a man's character and his fashion
of wearing his hair. "It was Grünewald's St. John who set
me free," he wrote later.

Other details of the Isenheimer Altar entranced him. He
was delighted with the devils and the fantastic animals in
the panel showing the Temptation of St. Antony. St. Antony
has been hurled down. One devil grips him by the hair,
another is about to tread him down. These devils are owls
wearing the carapaces of lizards, cocks twisted into the
shape of scorpions, horned griffins, bloated frog faces. There

is a terrifying power of devastation in the small, highly colored panel. Schweitzer remembers gazing at the Temptation of St. Antony, so fascinated that he could hardly tear himself away. Curiously, he does not remember a small inscription on the right of the panel, bearing the message which St. Antony scribbled at the moment before the devils assaulted him. This message, which could be regarded as in some way an emblem of all Schweitzer's later work in Africa, reads: *Ubi eras, bone Jhesu, ubi eras, quare non affuisti ut sanares vulnera mea?* "Where wert thou, good Jesus, where wert thou? Why didst thou not come to heal my wounds?"

It was to put an end to such anguished cries uttered by the natives of French Equatorial Africa that Schweitzer went out to Lambaréné. In those terrible words, hidden in the corner of the painting like a signature, was a nakedness of thought to which he was slowly approaching.

Five minutes walk from the museum, along the Kleberstrasse, lie the pleasant gardens known as the *Champs de Mars.* In the middle of the gardens there stood until the German occupation of 1940–1945 the bronze statue of Admiral Armand-Joseph Bruat, the commander of the French fleet during the Crimean War. At the base of the column were four figures representing the four corners of the earth, and the south was represented by a bronze Negro giant. The Negro's powerful head was bent in abject surrender, and yet there was a great nobility in the features. Whenever he visited the gardens with his godparents Schweitzer begged permission to make a little detour and bow his head before that amazing sculpture by Bartholdi.

When he wrote his reminiscences of Colmar, Schweitzer said simply: "It was this statue by Bartholdi which summoned me at the age of thirty to live and work in Africa." *

It was true, and not entirely true. Many other influences had been at work. There was the obscure missionary Casalis who wrote letters from his missionary station among the Bantus, urging French protestants to help their Negro brethren—once a month in his church Schweitzer's father delivered sermons on the subject of missionary endeavours and he was especially fond of Casalis. There was the example of his uncle, the saintly Pastor Albert Schillinger, the hero of Strasbourg. Then, too, there was the whole tradition of French protestantism, whose members regard themselves as an embattled *élite*, chosen by God to improve the lot of suffering mankind. French protestants have a long tradition of opposition to injustice. In 1870 it was the French protestant ministers who refused capitulation to the Prussian army. Throughout the eighteenth century French Protestantism had revolted against the secular powers and had refused to yield to torture. While the men went to the galleys, the women locked up in the beautiful Tower of Constance at Aigues-Mortes carved the word "RÉSISTER" on the stones of the prison floor. Schweitzer was the child of his church, and of his divided land, and of generations of simple educated men. It would never have occurred to him not to assume the largest burden.

But when he left the gymnasium at Mulhouse, he had not

* Today, the head of the Negro, all that remains of the statue, stands in Albert Schweitzer's small ground-floor study at Günsbach. The huge, beautifully carved face towers over everything else in the room.

yet chosen his future field. He knew only that he was dedicated to God, to music and to mankind. Before him lay twenty years of study before he sailed to the Ogowe river in Africa.

~~~ 4 ~~~

The Years of Apprenticeship

AT SOME TIME IN JULY OR
August 1893, shortly after Schweitzer had passed his final
examination at the Gymnasium in Mulhouse and when he
was preparing to enter Strasbourg University, a photograph
was taken of him. It is a strange and revealing photograph.
At first sight he looks dapper. He wears a small mustache,
his thick dark hair is neatly parted, the eyebrows are neatly
trimmed and the lips are pursed gently together in an expression which suggests nothing more than the usual sensual-
ity of a handsome youth aware of being handsome. He looks
in fact astonishingly like the son of a rich *commerçant*,
with a taste for the arts, hardly to be distinguished from
thousands of other college students, with an appealing man-
ner and a devotion to pleasure. Look closer and put a
finger over the mustache, and the gentle, sensual youth disappears: then immediately you are aware of the determination in the chin, the boldly rounded forehead and the steadi-
ness of the inquiring eyes, set far apart. Two people gaze
out from the photograph, and perhaps it was inevitable that
in the course of time they should wage war with one another.

That summer saw the end of his youth and the beginning
of his manhood. He had already decided what he wanted
to do with his life. He would study theology, philosophy and
music. Beyond that he knew little, but for the moment it
was sufficient; and through the long summer and well into
the autumn he gathered books around him and continued
his studies at Günsbach. He was about to go up to the
University of Strasbourg when he received an invitation
from his uncle Charles, his father's elder brother, to visit
Paris. He had never been there. He jumped at the invitation,
a reward for his good work at the Gymnasium, even though
it would be a visit of only a few weeks. He reached Paris
early in October, and had to be back in Strasbourg by the
end of the month.

He had expected to find a city seething with intellectual
ferment, but he found instead that Paris was given over to
the reign of pleasure. It was gay and noisy, and he refused
to be intimidated by gaiety and noise. He had the typical
provincial's disrespect for the capital. Paris, after all, was
only a pale imitation of Colmar. Even the Louvre could not
be compared with the Museum at Colmar, where the paintings of Grünewald and Schongauer crowded the walls. In-
tensely serious, he explored the city and wrote home that
there was absolutely nothing of any value there. Alarmed,
Aunt Mathilde suggested that he should at least view the
great organ in the church of St. Sulpice and meet the great
organist, Charles Marie Widor. Schweitzer agreed, and
armed with an introduction from Aunt Mathilde he set off
to the church.

It happened to be the day when Paris was celebrating the

Franco-Russian *rapprochement*. French regard for Russia and for the Tsar Alexander III was at its height. Russian sailors, under Admiral Avellan, were making a tour through the city and being cheered by everyone. Banners hung from the lampposts. Everywhere there were signs written in French and Russian. There were parades all day, and at night there were torchlight processions, with the white-uniformed Russian sailors everywhere. One morning Schweitzer fought his way through the crowds, and was late for the meeting with Widor, who sat patiently before the keyboard of the greatest organ in France, built thirty years before by the acknowledged expert, Aristide Cavaillé-Col. This huge organ had five manuals and over a hundred speaking stops. Widor, who had been elected Professor of Music at the Conservatoire at the age of twenty-five and was already at fifty regarded as the greatest of French composers for the organ, was a man of few words. As soon as Schweitzer appeared, he said: "What will you play?" Schweitzer answered: "I will play Bach." Thereupon he began to play as well as he had ever played in his life before.

Widor was a man who deliberately went out of his way to cultivate young musicians. Soon he was telling Schweitzer that he had never heard Bach played with such profundity, and he pointed out some of Schweitzer's technical deficiencies. He offered to make the young German his pupil without fee, and not content with this, went to great pains to make his new pupil's life in Paris enjoyable, giving him letters of introduction and sometimes, when he saw that the slender young provincial was not eating as regularly as he should—Schweitzer had made it a point of honor to spend

as little of his father's money as possible—they took their
meals together. Widor was at the top of the musical pro-
fession, Schweitzer at the bottom. But from the moment of
their first meeting until the day of Widor's death the friendship was close and heartwarming. When Schweitzer speaks,
as he does often, of the men to whom he is most indebted,
the name of Widor comes first.

By the end of October he was back in Strasbourg, being
interviewed by the faculty and preparing his courses. He
enjoyed Strasbourg, then as now a city given to that intense
intellectual effort which Schweitzer found inexplicably wanting in Paris. He liked the old quais by the river Ill, the winding streets full of timbered houses, the immense soaring
cathedral. Once French, in German hands since the Franco-
Prussian War, Strasbourg succeeded in combining French
grace with German solidity. The university, with its facul-
ties of protestant theology, law, letters and medicine, was
regarded as a leading institution of learning on both sides
of the Rhine. Schweitzer's main course was theology, and
he therefore took up residence in the theological college of
St. Thomas. Like all the students of his own age, he knew
he had only a few months of university study in front of
him: in the spring of the following year he would be drafted
into military service in the German army.

He worked hard. He had disliked learning Hebrew at the
Gymnasium, and had in fact learned very little. He still disliked it, and only with the greatest effort, working against
the grain, did he pass his preliminary examination in Hebrew. A few weeks later, with a Greek testament in his
haversack, he was taking part in maneuvers in Lower

Alsace. He was an unusual soldier. He obeyed orders implicitly, with the cunning of an automaton, but in the evenings, when the draftees were allowed a little leisure, he disappeared from sight. In whatever hiding-place he could find, he was poring over the commentaries written by his professor at the university, Dr. Heinrich Holtzmann, on the Synoptic Gospels. So he spent the summer, and one day in the autumn, his eyes falling on the tenth chapter of the *Gospel according to St. Matthew,* he read:

Behold, I send you forth as sheep in the midst of wolves: be ye therefore wise as serpents, and harmless as doves.
But beware of men: for they will deliver you up to the councils, and they will scourge you in their synagogues.
Think not that I have come to send peace on earth: I came not to send peace, but a sword.

Jesus is describing the mission of the Twelve, telling them what they must do during these last days when the Kingdom of Heaven is at hand. He promises them that persecution and terror will be their lot; and in verses of strained and terrifying majesty announces the Coming of the Messiah.

According to accepted protestant interpretation—an interpretation shared by Professor Holtzmann—this whole chapter consisted of a collection of "sayings of Jesus" uttered at different times and different places, for none of the things that Jesus said were about to happen did happen. The Messiah did not come at this time. There was no persecution and no terror. Pondering this terrible chapter, Schweitzer concluded that it meant exactly what it said: that Jesus had sent the Twelve on their mission, believing that the

Kingdom of Heaven was at hand and that the last days
were upon the world; and believing this, he was fallible, for
the Kingdom of Heaven was still far removed from men.
If the words were taken literally, and he could see no reason
for taking them in any other way, the fallibility of Jesus
must be accepted.

In the following chapter Schweitzer's eyes fell upon another crux. Jesus says:

Verily I say unto you, Among them that are born of women
there hath not risen a greater than John the Baptist: notwith-
standing, he that is least in the Kingdom of Heaven is greater
than he.

Protestant commentators had for long argued that Jesus
was indicating that his own followers were more highly
regarded by God than the Baptist who had led the way.
Schweitzer wondered how this could be possible, since the
Baptist was the forerunner, the Elijah who prepares the way
for the coming of the Messiah. So he argued that the
words should be interpreted in the sense that his own followers had become through the dawn of the Messianic Kingdom spiritual beings, while the Baptist, who came before
the dawn, remained "a man born of woman" even though
he assumed the role of Elijah. Yet the Baptist possessed a
unique greatness, surpassing that of all other human beings,
in that he became a member of the Kingdom of Heaven
while remaining a man.

With these two interpretations Schweitzer began to lay
the foundations of his theological researches, which culmi-
nated in the most important of his books, *The Quest of the*

Historical Jesus. This book will be described later. Here it is sufficient to say that Schweitzer opened out an entire new field of theological research and succeeded, where most theologians had failed, in giving a continuous portrait of the historical Jesus. He explained without "explaining away" nearly all the difficult *cruces*, and he showed that the fallibility of Jesus did not in the least detract from his divinity.

All this was seed-time; the harvest came later. Outwardly Schweitzer resembled most of the other young theological students, and he did not discuss his lurking doubts over the accepted theological interpretations with Professor Holtzmann. In one respect, however, he differed from his fellow students. While engrossed in philosophy and theology, he was also engrossed in music.

He was studying music as though he had a whole lifetime to give to it. Ernst Münch, the brother of his teacher in Mulhouse, was organist at St. Wilhelm's church in Strasbourg, close to the university. Ernst was far more explosive and exacting than his more famous brother, but he was an equally gifted teacher. Schweitzer had his last lesson from Eugen in August 1893 shortly before the journey to Paris, and he had his first lesson with Ernst a few days after entering the theological school. It pleased him that the continuity was maintained. Soon he was being regarded as a part of Ernst's intimate family—they were spending longer and longer hours over the dining-room table arranging for concerts and devoutly wishing they could perform all of Bach's cantatas "altogether and at once." Strasbourg was Bach-conscious. St. Wilhelm's church choir and the municipal orchestra had formed an alliance, and with Eugen Münch summoned from Mulhouse, or with Schweitzer at the organ, and with all the resources of the municipal orchestra, the *St. Matthew Passion* and the *B Minor Mass* were played with wonderful effect. Inevitably there were difficulties. The concerts were free, and no one ever knew until the last moment how the expenses would be met. There was trouble, too, with the music-critics, until it was discovered that if they sat bunched together they usually wrote disapproving reviews, but if they were widely separated they wrote enthusiastically. Schweitzer himself wrote the preliminary accounts for the concerts. They were enormously lengthy, but the newspapers were hungry for articles on music and printed them in full even when they were long enough to fill whole pages.

Though Schweitzer was already one of the leaders of the Bach cult in Strasbourg, he was far from being satisfied with studying Bach alone. He attended the municipal opera and plunged deep in its repertoire of Mozart, Gluck and Wagner. He had no patience with the enthusiasts of Bach who decried Wagner. For him Wagner was the supreme dramatic lyricist, the equal of Bach and Beethoven. Fifty years later he wrote from Africa that Wagner was above all musicians unique in his consummate understanding of the resources of each instrument and the most gifted in creating a grandiose musical architecture. He yearned for dramatic power on the stage, and found it characteristically in the performance of Heinrich Vogl who played the role of Loki, the fire god, in *Das Rheingold*. Vogl avoided the pyrotechnics of the modern Wagnerian actor. He did not dance round the stage in time with the music, or wear harlequin costume. It was enough that he wore his fiery red cloak, restlessly swinging it from one shoulder to the other, in no other way attracting attention to himself. And Schweitzer, after commenting on Vogl's performance at length, vividly remembering every detail, commented: "He showed himself to be the furious power of destruction among the gods as they marched all unsuspecting to their fatal sunset." It is a sentence worth pondering. In the original German it comes with tremendous force and emphasis. It could be written only by a man following in the high Romantic tradition. And here and there in Schweitzer's writings we shall come upon these passages of fire and thunder which are oddly at variance with his usual quiet and chiseled philosophical prose.

Schweitzer saw Heinrich Vogl's performance for the first time in 1896, during his third year at the university. His uncle Charles, pleased with his progress in musical studies, had sent him from Paris tickets for the performance of *The Ring of the Nibelungs* at Bayreuth. By stinting himself to one meal a day, he was able to save enough money for the railway fare. The first complete performance of the *Ring* cycle took place in August, 1876. Now twenty years later came the second, and Schweitzer was there to applaud it. He even caught a glimpse of Cosima Wagner, the daughter of Liszt, an imperious woman who some years later included him among her acquaintances. She was by turns gentle and forbidding with him, and sometimes discussed theological questions with him on long summer walks beside the Ill river. He admired her, but could never bring himself to feel affection for her, for "she liked to have people approach her with the reverence due to a princess." Schweitzer possessed considerable diplomatic skill. He had employed it frequently when he was acting as mediator between Ernst Münch and the treasurer of St. Wilhelm's church; both were fiery-tempered. But Cosima Wagner's coldness was like the coldness of steel, and he was ill-at-ease when invited to the Villa Wahnfried. "I would have preferred," he said, "to go out into the country and sit down by myself."

Returning from Bayreuth to Strasbourg, he left the train at Stuttgart to see the new organ which had been installed in the Liederhalle. The instrument was famous for its pure tones and its modern construction. Schweitzer listened to a Bach fugue played on the new organ and was dumbfounded. He had expected to be able to distinguish the separate voices and he expected purity, and he found neither. This he called "my Damascus at Stuttgart." All his life he had played on magnificent organs. How was it, he asked, that a new expensive organ should be so much worse than those he had played? He was to learn that the art of organ-building was on the wane. He decided to make a careful study of organ-building and to devote a good part of his time examining organs all over Europe. The experience bore fruit a decade later when he wrote a comprehensive manual on organ construction.

He was twenty-one. He had discovered Wagner. He had discovered in himself a talent for philosophy and an understanding of theology. What remained? How would he live his life? What would he do with these gifts which he possessed in such abundance? These questions he had already asked himself at Whitsuntide. He remembered waking from a deep sleep. He was at home, at Günsbach. The sunlight streamed through the leaves around the window. The scent of apple-blossom and lilac came into the quiet room. He heard birdsong, and the wind brought the sound of someone practicing the organ, and soon came the church bells. Why had God given him vigorous health, a family he loved, prodigious talents? Sometimes pride had assailed him. He had seen himself exerting all his talents to the uttermost, acquiring a great fame. To what end? So now he asked himself quite calmly what the purpose of his life should be. It was not enough to enjoy his strength; he must share it with others. But how? He did not know. But he knew that the time for sharing would come. When? He decided to give himself nine more years. During that time he would exert all his skills, demonstrate all his powers to the uttermost. At the age of thirty he would abandon them, following the demand of Jesus: "Whosoever shall save his life shall lose it, and whosoever shall lose his life for My sake and the Gospels shall save it." He did not know how he would accomplish that exacting demand, but when he got out of bed, his mind was made up. There remained nine years of intellectual activity, and all the rest of his life was to be dedicated to the service of humanity.

With renewed energy, he threw himself into his studies. He read voluminously, passed his first theological examination, studied musical scores, played the organ and prepared for his doctorate in philosophy. These years he was living in a room in the Old Fish Market, down by the embankment. He did not know it at the time, but later he learned that he had been occupying the room which had belonged to Goethe in the days when he was writing his first sketch of the Faust play.

Paris called him. Towards the end of 1898 he decided to transfer to the Sorbonne. Here he intended to write a thesis on the religious philosophy of Kant and continue to study the organ under Widor, who was to become his collaborator as well as his teacher. Widor had been puzzled by Bach's sudden changes of mood. Inexplicably in the chorale preludes Bach passed quickly from one idea to another, and from the chromatic to the diatonic scale. Schweitzer was able to explain to him that Bach was simply following the order of the old Lutheran texts. Widor, who had imagined that Bach had been writing in pure counterpoint, was amazed. He had not imagined there would be any simple explanation for a problem which had disturbed him over many years, and he insisted that Schweitzer think about producing an edition of Bach which would carry the poetry above the interpreting music. And was there anywhere to be found a study of Bach's symbolism, the particular value he places on poetry? Finding there was no such study, Widor hinted that Schweitzer was exactly the man to do it. Thus was born the great two-volume study of Bach, which appeared eight years later.

At first Schweitzer quailed before the prospect of writing it. It had seemed so easy: all that was needed was a study of Bach's poetry. But the poetry of the chorales was inextricably involved with the poetry of the cantatas, and then of the Masses; and to interpret the texts more fully, it would be necessary to interpret Bach also. When Schweitzer said

plaintively that there was no end to the work of interpreting
Bach, Widor answered: "Quite right, but there is nothing
you cannot do if you have the order and the desire."

That autumn and spring he was living in the shadow of
the Sorbonne, but he rarely attended lectures. He worked
with Widor, took piano lessons and wrote his thesis on
Kant. It was a bad winter, with the Seine flooded, and
though he was to make many visits to Paris later, he always
tried to avoid those harsh winter days when the ice-cold
winds blow down the boulevards. In future he decided he
would try to visit Paris in the spring; during the autumn
holidays he would return to Günsbach.

From Strasbourg University he had received a small scholarship which allowed him to study wherever he desired.
When spring came round, he decided to study in Berlin. He
found the intellectual life of Paris little to his taste; in Berlin
he found that deep seriousness he desired, finding it especially in the household of the distinguished archeologist and
hellenist Ernst Curtius. One day in the summer of 1899 he
was in Curtius's house when some scholars gathered together to discuss a paper which had just been read before
the Academy of Science. Schweitzer was not particularly
attentive until he heard someone saying in tones of disgust:
"Ach was! Wir sind ja doch alle nur Epigonen!" "Look
here, we are only inheritors of the past!" When Schweitzer
returned home that night, his head was on fire. It seemed to
him quite suddenly and with blinding clarity that this unknown scholar had expressed a deep truth. Modern European culture had no existence of its own; it survived on the
glory of its past. He determined then and there to write a

book to be called *Wir Epigonen*—"We, the Inheritors"—
and though the book was never written, there are long chapters in *The Philosophy of Civilization* he wrote later, and
whole paragraphs in the speech he delivered on acceptance
of the Nobel Prize which can be traced back to that moment
of realization one summer evening in Berlin at the turn of
the century.

In those days Berlin still possessed an engaging provincial
appearance; its university was one of the greatest in the
world. Paris was being torn apart over the Dreyfus case; in
Berlin there was vigorous confidence and a sense of permanence. But the city was lacking in good organs, and
Schweitzer complained there were no organs there to be
compared with Widor's organ at St. Sulpice or the organ in
the Cathedral of Nôtre Dame.

Berlin was so satisfying that he made arrangements to
return. Meanwhile he had to return to Strasbourg to take
the examination for his doctorate in philosophy. He did so
well that his Professor, Theodor Ziegler, urged him to become a *privat-dozent* in philosophy. But already he had his
doctorate in theology and now he was determined to continue his theological studies and take his licenciate in theology, which is a grade higher than a doctorate and would
offer him the rank of a full professor. There were other
reasons why he refused to embrace a philosophical career.
He felt a great need to preach. It was a need he had inherited
from his father, and as a *privat-dozent* or even as a full
professor of philosophy, the university authorities would
hardly welcome a preacher in their ranks. He was still
immersed in biblical studies, and he was contemplating a

long stay in one of the English universities. But on December
1, 1899, he became organist at the Church of St. Nicholas,
where his uncle Albert Schillinger had been curate. Here he
worked on a study of the Last Supper and another study on
the Passion and Messiahship of Jesus. He was glad he had
put philosophy away. Now his life revolved around the two
poles of music and theology. By July 1900 he received his
licentiate in theology with his study of the Last Supper, passing his examination "magna cum laude"; then he was free
to become a curate. His stipend was 100 marks ($20) a
month, but it was enough for his needs. His superiors were
two ministers of widely different beliefs: one was a liberal,
the other a pietistic orthodox follower of the Lutheran
church. It delighted Schweitzer that in spite of their theological differences, they should behave towards each other
with so much brotherly affection.

Other things delighted him. His passion for preaching
now had full rein. Because he was shy, he preferred the
afternoon services where there were only a few worshippers;
then he could address them intimately, as his father ad-
dressed the small intimate congregations at Günsbach. He
would revise his sermons endlessly, writing them out in full,
but as likely as not he would throw the completed sermon
away when it came to facing his audience. These afternoon
sermons he regarded as simple devotional exercises, sometimes quite brief. Their brevity alarmed some of the parish-
ioners, and the matter was taken up with the minister.
Schweitzer said: "I am just a poor curate who stops speaking
when he has nothing more to say." He was solemnly but
kindly reproved, and told that in future he must never speak

for less than twenty minutes. Best of all he enjoyed the Confirmation classes he took three times a week.

As a curate he was allowed spring and autumn vacations, and now he could put into practice his desire to spend the spring in Paris and the autumn in Günsbach. The brief summer holiday he spent in Germany, watching the Oberammergau Passion Play with Aunt Mathilde. He was more impressed by the mountains behind Oberammergau than by the play, though he acknowledged that the village players were authentic actors, not overspoiled by the adulation they had received. But the banality of the texts and the music annoyed him, and he could not easily get over their wooden delivery. Aunt Mathilde was her usual sprightly self. She informed him that she had invited him to make the journey through Bavaria because she wanted someone to look after the baggage. In fact, she wanted him for his companionship. She was herself an excellent pianist, with a wide knowledge of music, and so it was inevitable that they should go on to Bayreuth and pay their respects to Cosima Wagner, who greeted them kindly, if a little coldly. At Bayreuth, too, Schweitzer enjoyed some conversations with Houston Stewart Chamberlain, a fanatic racist to whom Hitler admitted a great debt. Schweitzer was impressed by Chamberlain's vast erudition and was inclined to agree with his explosive analysis of the Russian character: even today Schweitzer considers the Russians as "semi-Asiatics." Soon he was back in Strasbourg, and when the principal of the theological school died, the governors of the college decided to make Schweitzer the acting principal. At the age of 26 he was a marked man, learned in music, philosophy and theology.

Now for the first time he had to exert his administrative abilities.

That winter he was working prodigiously hard. He was working on the study of Bach for Widor, he was contemplating a vast study of the history of civilization in terms of its philosophy, and he had written out and given as lectures an outline of the life of Jesus, which he hoped one day to publish. In addition he had embarked on a work to be called *A History of the Last Supper and Baptism in Early Christian Times.* He was organist, curate and acting principal of a college, but these were not his only burdens. For many years, ever since he came to Strasbourg as a student, he had thrown himself into social work as a member of the student association known as the Diaconate of St. Thomas. Money was collected, and students were sent out on their bicycles to interview the poor and sick, to find out how much money they needed and to be sure that they were in sore straits. Schweitzer, like the other students, also had to collect money. He detested begging, and showed no marked gift for it, though in later years he was glad he was introduced into the techniques of begging when he was still quite young—there was so very much begging to do later. As acting principal, and later as principal, he continued his social work, and began to take an interest in vagrants and discharged prisoners. He was still looking for that work to which he could offer himself completely, and for a while he thought it might be among the derelicts of Alsace. He thought briefly of working among abandoned and destitute children. In Alsace there were as yet no social workers. Perhaps, he thought, in some way not yet clear to him, he

might find his task—the task to which he would surrender
his life—among these forgotten children. It was 1903. In
two years, if he obeyed his promise to himself, he would
have to make his great decision. He had still not found what
he was searching for, and he was beginning to be impatient.

Among the students who regularly accompanied the
members of the Diaconate of St. Thomas on their social
work was a young, dark-haired and pretty Jewish girl called
Hélène Bresslau, the daughter of the famous Strasbourg historian, Harry Bresslau, editor-in-chief of the great collection
of mediaeval German documents known as the *Monumenta
Germaniae Historica.* Intense and high-spirited, Hélène
Bresslau, unknown to Schweitzer, had made the same kind
of promise. She would live for herself until the age of
twenty-five, and then offer herself to suffering humanity.
She had taken up nursing. And she was impressed by
Schweitzer. He could ask for no one better to share with him
the perilous course he had set for himself, and when he left
for Paris during the summer of 1903 there was already a
tacit agreement between them that they would get married.

In Paris Schweitzer returned to his old haunts. Widor was
still vigorously alive. Unhappily Cavaillé-Col, the man who
built the St. Sulpice organ, was dead: he had died in great
poverty, leaving nothing to his family, having spent all the
money he ever earned on building his magnificent organs.
But that summer he heard Wanda Landowska play Bach on
the harpsichord. It was another revelation, and he offered
her his enthusiastic support.

In Strasbourg he had long ago abandoned the large room
on Old Fish Market. He lived now in the splendor of his

official quarters—five large and sunny rooms on the second floor of the College of St. Thomas, overlooking the embankment. His stipend was now 2,000 marks ($400) a year. IIe could count on receiving royalties from his books, and he was able to make comparatively large sums of money giving organ recitals. But the work which absorbed him most was *The Quest of the Historical Jesus,* which took him four years to write. The work involved the study of all the lives of Jesus which had appeared in the last three centuries—he introduces 67 separate lives in the first edition of the book, and studied a round dozen more in the second edition—and as he read these lives, and all the attendant studies, borrowing books in great armfuls from the college library—the librarian was continually finding for him more and more illustrative documents, more articles in obscure magazines and more pamphlets—Schweitzer was almost drowned in books. For each particular author there was a large pile. The study was invaded by great columns of books, all carefully arranged for Schweitzer's convenience. Visitors had to make their way as best they could among the tottering columns, and his Württemburg housekeeper almost suffered from apoplexy. Schweitzer gave her strict orders to sweep around the books, but never under them. So the months passed, and the leaning towers grew larger rather than smaller, and there seemed no end in sight to this prolonged examination of the lives of Jesus written mostly by German authors: there was hardly a life which was not a vast two-volume compendium: and Schweitzer was determined to read through all of them, making careful notes, evaluating one life against another, until he could have almost recited all the volumes by heart.

In the autumn of 1904, the work was nearly over. Another year, and the end would be in sight. One evening, as he was working in his study, he glanced idly at the green-covered magazine of the Paris Missionary Society, which reported every month on the progress of its missions in Senegal, Tahiti, New Caledonia, Madagascar and the Gabon in French Equatorial Africa. This slim magazine, printed on thin paper, was familiar to Schweitzer. He had read many issues, and always avidly. His father for many years had taken out a subscription to the magazine, and some of the letters written to the editor by missionaries in far-flung colonies were read out from the pulpit in Günsbach during the missionary services which occurred once a month. Recently, Schweitzer had had little time to read the magazine. He was about to put it aside after mechanically turning the pages, when his eyes fell on the title of an article on the needs of the Congo Mission written by Alfred Boegner, the president of the Paris Missionary Society, and like Schweitzer, an Alsatian.

It was a brief article of no more than four pages. The article told of natives suffering atrociously in the hands of the witch-doctors. Alfred Boegner painted a picture of the forests and the rivers of the northern territory of the French Congo: the unimaginable suffering which goes on, deep in the interior. He begged for Christian workers to go out there, and he urged that someone "on whom the Master's eyes already rested" would make the decision of dedicating himself to this urgent work. "Men and women who can reply simply to the Master's call, 'Lord, I am coming,' these are the people the Church needs." These were the last words of the article, and having read them, Schweitzer quietly closed the magazine and went on with his work. He knew his search was over.

A few months later came his thirtieth birthday. He was still principal of the theological college, but he was living in a strange unreal world. He made decisions, gave orders, supervised the work of the college, and all the time he was aware that he was living on borrowed time. His mind was somewhere in the interior of Africa, but he was still counting the cost. His books were unfinished. He could complete them first, and then set out for the Equator. More than anything else he had been impressed by Alfred Boegner's account of the diseases suffered by the natives. There were almost no doctors. Sleeping sickness was rampant. There were diseases of the skin more terrible than any in Europe. If he was to live among the natives, he could not go as a teacher or as a missionary alone. More and more he saw that he would have no excuse for going unless he first became a medical doctor.

He told no one except Hélène Bresslau about his plan. At first the whole conception of the plan shocked him. It was not that in any way he refused to face "the surrender to Africa"; it was simply that if he went as a doctor, he would have to spend a period of six or seven years in medical studies. And yet he could see no alternative. It was all very well for his theological friends to deliver fine sermons, saying that the Christian must surrender to the will of Christ. The words were satisfying, and usually the words could be interpreted in terms of a small, even a miniscule sacrifice. Christ demanded that one should be charitable: a few pennies

given to a beggar sufficiently answered the need. But to
surrender books, and the writing of them, and organs, and
the playing of them; to surrender a high theological position; to go out and spread God's word by a skill he did not
yet possess; to break the close link which bound him to the
Rhine and the Black Forest and the Vosges Mountains—all
this was like a crushing blow on the face. He attacked the
problem cautiously, like the man in the parable who "desir-
ing to build a tower, first counts the cost whether he have
wherewith to complete it." He was prepared to make minor
compromises. He would complete his book on Bach and the
book of studies on the lives of Jesus. So another year
passed, and it was not until October 13, 1906, that he
dropped into a letter-box in the Avenue de la Grande Armée
in Paris a handful of letters to his parents and close acquaintances, saying that at the beginning of the winter semester he
would enter Strasbourg University as a medical student.
He added that he was determined to spend the greater part
of what remained of his life as a doctor in Equatorial
Africa.

In Berlin, Paris, Strasbourg and Günsbach the letters were
received with indignation. Widor was appalled, saying it
was an act of crass folly. "You are like a brilliant general
who exposes himself as a common soldier on the front line,"
Widor said. Romain Rolland said little, but his words were
interpreted by Schweitzer to mean that he could neither
approve nor disapprove. Few encouraged him; nearly everyone thought he had suddenly gone mad. The burden of their
letters was: "You are throwing up a great career on a whim.
If you are disappointed at the slow growth of your reputa-

tion, be humble and patient—you will soon be recognized. Above all, stay where your roots are!" Someone suggested he was exiling himself to Africa as the result of an unfortunate love affair. His motives were examined from all angles, and usually found wanting. Especially absurd seemed his desire to go to Africa as a doctor, not as a preacher, for he had spent thirty years of his life in a laborious apprenticeship to theology. A lady who had earned Schweitzer's gratitude for her wisdom in the past suggested that it would be much simpler if he stayed in Europe, gave lectures and organ recitals on behalf of the natives of Equatorial Africa, and so followed the dictates of his conscience without doing harm to his career. Schweitzer was stung by these responses. Widor had treated him like a son, and it was Widor's letter which hurt him most. And he felt a curious dread about the project. He was not at all sure he would succeed as a medical missionary, or that any missionary organization would accept him, or that he was strong enough to sustain the backbreaking burden of seven years of medical study. To venture upon such a project, he felt, a man must be prepared for disaster—even the ultimate disaster of dying quite early in his medical career in the African forest. But what disturbed him more than anything else was the bitterness of the letters he received, and the astonishing way in which people decried his motives and tore open the doors and windows of his soul.

By October 1906 he had been living with the project for a whole year. He had explored every facet of the problem. Cold-bloodedly, he had examined himself from every conceivable angle. Though Goethe's philosophy was largely his own, he did not see himself as a Faustian figure; he was not "one of the restless ones forever wandering across the earth"; and he did not demand of himself an exhibition of superhuman heroism. *Im Anfang war die Tat.* "In the beginning was the deed." So Goethe had said, and Schweitzer was weary of intellectual pursuits unrelated to the facts of common humanity. For him it was particularly significant that Goethe had made Wilhelm Meister come at the end of his wanderings to see that the doctor's life was the best and most fruitful.

In later years Schweitzer was to say: "I wanted to be a doctor so that I might work without having to talk." It was only half of the truth, but it was an important half. In fact, he wanted to be a doctor because he had awakened one morning in Günsbach to see the sunlight pouring in his window, and at that instant he had vowed to dedicate his life to humanity, and only by becoming a doctor in Central Africa could he see himself assuming a *responsible* burden. It was above all important to find a vocation worthy of a man's self-surrender: it must be hard, purposeful, unrelenting. This he had found, and from the moment when he put the letters into the postbox in the Avenue de la Grande Armée, he knew no doubts.

In the spring of 1906 his resignation of the principalship of the Theological School was accepted. By good fortune the president of the Superior Consistory and the legal owner of the theological school buildings was Friedrich Curtius, the son of the famous Ernst Curtius he had known well in Berlin. So it happened that Schweitzer was allowed to remain in the School. Instead of the large rooms on the second floor overlooking the embankment, he was given three small rooms and a kitchen in the attic. It was raining on Shrove Tuesday when some students, superintended by Schweitzer, began to haul his possessions out of the front door and then carry them through a side-door to the small rooms under the gable roof.

The little cluttered rooms in the roof symbolised the change in his fortunes. The power and the glory had departed. Now there was to be unremitting work "in the service of the spiritual and the true," with the possibility of failure awaiting him at every turn.

The Young Doctor

"NEVER HAVE I KNOWN SUCH
fatigue as I knew in those days," Schweitzer wrote later.

It was a fatigue which seemed to have no end, and no
surcease; it attended him during the lectures at the Medical
Faculty, during his walks and during his reading. His mind,
long geared to thinking in abstract terms, was now compelled
to deal with a thousand details of practical zoology and
physiology. He was working under intense strain in an en-
vironment totally unfamiliar to him, among men whose
minds moved easily among the realities of test tubes and
microscopes, who saw everything clearly and simply and
were in no way distracted by the scruples which come from
a study of the humanities. For years Schweitzer had lived
among the apocryphal prophets who wrote of the promise
of a Messianic Kingdom, his greatest contribution to the
study of Jesus being his insistence that Jesus must be seen
in terms of the apocalyptic time in which He lived. Enoch,
Baruch and Ezra, Jewish poets of soaring imaginations,
were his constant companions. Almost he dwelt amid the
flames of the Last Day. Now it was winter in Strasbourg,

drab classrooms, the lecturers' voices droning on, the Bunsen burners on the long benches, the acid smell which haunts all medical buildings. Then, as now, German universities offered hard regimens and a student is expected to devote eighteen hours a day to his work. He had enjoyed the freedom which comes to a man who is the principal of a college; now, at the age of thirty-one, he was suffering the slavery of being a student. Within six months he was exhausted and on the verge of a nervous breakdown.

It was largely his own fault. While working at his medical studies, he continued with his books. In the winter of 1906 he wrote a long essay on organ-building and completed the last chapter of *The Quest of the Historical Jesus,* which contains his best writing, though it shows signs of intolerable strain. He slept little, and sometimes forgot to eat. When the strain became altogether intolerable, he would slip into St. Wilhelm's church, to play Bach for an hour with Ernst Münch. Then the weariness vanished, and he was calm again.

He was taking risks with his health which would have appalled a man who did not have his peasant strength. He was prepared to offer himself to Africa, but he was not yet prepared to surrender his gifts. He went on writing his books, he continued to give organ concerts, he was still the pastor of St. Nicholas and he still lectured on theology. He had completed the book on Bach promised to Widor. It had been written in French—Hélène Bresslau observed that he sometimes wrote French with German idioms and helped him to correct them—and now he was asked to translate the book into German for a German publisher. But when he

sat down to the task, he realised that he would have to write
the book in an entirely different way for a German audience,
so he sat down to write a new book on Bach. And now that
he had completed a study of all the lives of Jesus, he began
to prepare notes for a similar study of St. Paul.

The tasks he set himself were inexhaustible, but he added
to them at leisure. He was already regarded as one of the
great authorities on organ-building, and was continually
being asked to give his views on organs. This meant traveling away from Strasbourg and giving up time he could
barely afford. He still visited Paris frequently during the
holidays—he was being received in the salons of Countess
Mélanie de Pourtelès and of Princess Metternich—but he
came to Paris to give concerts which would pay for his university fees, and this meant spending the previous day at
rehearsals. He learned to take short naps in the middle of
the day and to sleep easily on trains. He was punishing himself to the utmost, and vastly enjoying, in his rare moments
of tranquility, his capacity to squander himself in so many
directions.

He had made on unexpected discovery. When he entered
medical school, he thought he was deliberately resigning
himself to a world of facts. In time he came to regard the
long hours spent in the study of anatomy and physiology as
part of a continuing spiritual experience. It gave him more
than knowledge; it gave him a sense of the world outside
himself, that reflection of the universal Being which exists
outside men's minds. It was raw, naked and ugly, but it was
part of the truth. He refused to surrender the primacy of
the mind. But he saw that the historians and philosophers

were too often remote from reality. There was even a kind of intoxicated delight which came from "dealing with realities which can be determined with exactitude." The study of medicine came in time to engross him, but he could not prevent himself from regretting that he no longer possessed the supple brain and phenomenal memory he possessed fifteen years before. Compared with the other students, he suffered from serious disadvantages.

One of the more serious of these disadvantages came from his growing affection for the natural sciences. He was so happy with them that he almost forgot to pay attention to the fact that he would soon be asked to sit for an examination. Only at the last moment did he have the good sense to join a cramming club, where students carefully examined questions set in past years and came to predict the questions and required answers for this year.

In September 1911 he played the organ in a performance of Widor's *Simphonia Sacra* in Munich, and in the next month he sat for his final medical examination, paying his fees out of the money he had received in Munich. The examination was lengthy and not completed until December 17th. "Then," he wrote later, "I strode from the hospital into the darkness of a winter evening, and I still could not grasp the fact that the terrible strain of the medical course was now over. Again and again I had to tell myself I was really awake and not dreaming. I was walking with my examiner, the surgeon Madelung, and his voice seemed to be coming to me from another world altogether. He was saying: 'It is only because you have such wonderful health you have been able to get through it.' "

There remained now only a year of practical work as an interne, and a doctoral thesis; then he would be free to go to Africa. He chose for his doctoral thesis a dissertation on the psychiatry of Jesus, carefully evaluating the various psychiatric theories which had been advanced to explain the personality of Jesus. He came to the conclusion that Jesus was never out of touch with reality and reacted at all times in a perfectly normal way. Though the book was short—the final version amounted to no more than 43 pages—Schweitzer found it difficult to write, and more than once nearly abandoned the effort. The book shows signs of strain, and of all his writings is the least rewarding, because in the effort to show that Jesus never suffered from paranoia or any other psychical disturbance, he succeeds in clothing Jesus in a garment of excessive normality. The last chapters of *The Quest of the Historical Jesus*, also written in a state of intense fatigue, show Jesus vibrant and ringing with life; the brief *Psychiatric Study of Jesus* shows Him behaving at all moments calmly and in full control of Himself, as He wanders happily through the landscape of the commonplace. In the effort to prove Jesus normal, he only succeeds in proving He was dull.

Now the worst was over. The long years of devotion to medicine had given him many new skills. If he was not pleased with his knowledge of surgery, he knew he was above the ordinary run of students in his knowledge of pharmacology. There was still a good deal to be learned. He travelled to Paris to take a course in tropical medicine and to make arrangements for the journey to Africa. Characteristically, he had left many important questions to the last.

From the very beginning he had wanted to serve under the Paris Missionary Society, but he had made little effort to contact the Mission Board. Now it was time to contact them. He found them strangely diffident. He was reminded that he was a German citizen whose well-known theological views were opposed by many, if not all, of the missionaries in the field. He offered to equip a small hospital at Lambaréné at his own expense. He promised to serve as a doctor, and only as a doctor, leaving to the other missionaries the task of proselytizing the natives. Again there were raised eyebrows. He pleaded. He was ordered to attend a meeting of the governing board to present his views. He refused. He knew exactly what would happen. Outnumbered, confronted by men determined to oppose him, he would have no opportunity to win them over, for they would question him on theological grounds where he was vulnerable. He decided to visit the members in their houses and press his case. A few of the members of the governing board greeted him with chilly politeness and sent him on his way. When he repeated his promise that he would take no part in preaching, but would remain *muet comme une carpe* (silent like a carp), they began to tolerate him; and when he said further that he would accept no salary, for he hoped to be able to live on his royalties, they offered him a moderate blessing, provided he did nothing to cause offence to the missionaries in the field. Many remained dubious over the appointment, but only one member of the governing board sent in his resignation in protest.

There were still more hurdles to cross. As a doctor with a German degree, he was prohibited from practicing in

France or in the French possessions overseas. Friends intervened. From German and French universities there poured affidavits testifying to his extraordinary aptitude for work in Equatorial Africa. Armed with these, the French Secretary of the Colonies was able to make an exception to the general rule.

Schweitzer celebrated the last victory by returning to Strasbourg and marrying Hélène Bresslau, who had been waiting patiently for nearly ten years for this moment. The marriage took place on June 18, 1912.

He was almost ready to leave for Africa. All that he needed now was enough money to keep the hospital going for about two years. He calculated he would need about $5,000, to maintain the hospital, and a roughly similar sum to pay for the drugs and equipment he would take with him. Some of this money he raised himself by giving concerts; for the rest he depended upon his friends. He had never been a good beggar, and as he went around Strasbourg asking for contributions to the hospital at Lambaréné, he was aware of his strange incapacity to beg without feeling obscurely ashamed. There were long days when he seemed to be rebuffed at every turn. Happily, his friends and students came to the rescue, and by October most of the money had been raised and he was busy checking accounts and deliveries of drugs, bandages, surgical instruments, kitchenware.

Up to this time he had little knowledge of finance. Now he had to learn how to prepare a medical budget; he had to know something about banking and customs duties and sailing rules. At first these tasks rankled. He was especially annoyed in dealing with chemists' catalogues, which were ill-arranged and seemed to have been compiled "by some porter's wife." In time he learned to delight in the making of neat lists of drugs and equipment. "I came to see that these material affairs should be carried on in a spirit of dedication," he wrote later. "Today, when I compile these lists of things to be ordered, setting them out in their proper order, I am aware of an artistic satisfaction."

There were so many lists to be prepared, so many people to be visited, so much money to be raised that in the end he fell ill. Once more he was haunted by that exhaustion which came over him whenever he had drained his strength. The journey to Africa was postponed until the winter was over. Though ill, he continued to write, and that winter he completed a revision of his book on *The Quest of the Historical Jesus*. It was a major revision, and his final word on the subject of the historicity of Jesus. The book, which has never been translated into English, contains two hundred more pages than the first edition and surveys the field with astonishing comprehensiveness. Everything is there, and the long story of attempts to write the life of Jesus is brought completely up to date. As he wrote the last words, he expected he would never again write any books on theological subjects. He had made his decision. He was prepared to make a complete surrender of himself to Africa, abandoning the organ, abandoning teaching and abandoning his financial independence; he would abandon his love of books and his passion for theological argument. In the end he abandoned none of these things, but in those early months of 1913 the deliberate intention was clear.

In February 1913 he sent seventy packing cases by goods

train to Bordeaux. Then he was ready. There remained only a last round of visits in Strasbourg and one last journey to Günsbach to see his ageing parents. Then on the afternoon of Good Friday, with the church bells echoing in his ears, he stood in the last compartment of the last railway coach and waved farewell to his native village. He was waving farewell to all of his past and to all the things which had been closest to his heart. He was thirty-eight, and at the beginning of a new career.

On Easter Day in Paris he played, with Widor beside him, the organ at St. Sulpice for the last time. And in Paris he received the famous lead-lined piano, weighing three tons, which the Bach Society presented to him for his long years of service to Bach in France. He was overwhelmed by the gesture, and deeply perturbed. He had sworn to put music behind him. Now, insidiously, music was returning to his life. He promised himself he would play the piano only rarely and as a relaxation. Never again except on infrequent journeys to Europe would he employ all his art in a performance. A crowd followed him to the Quai d'Orsay. Soon he was on his way to Bordeaux. It was a beautiful spring afternoon, offering promise for the future.

He was hardly on board the *Europe*, which was to take him to Africa, when the weather changed. Fog curdled over the ship; the heavy waves of the Bay of Biscay broke over the rails. In the middle of a Biscay storm, he could only watch and pray and hope that the cargo of medicines and drugs piled into the hatches at the last moment would survive the fury of the storm. He lay in his bunk, watching his luggage crashing from one side of his stateroom to the other;

it amused him to count the intervals between the roll of the ship and the crash of the luggage, for there was nothing he could do about it, and he had long ago learned to take comfort from little things. He was seasick, and for three days had hardly anything to eat. But at Teneriffe it was calm, and the passengers began to emerge from their hiding-places.

He liked Teneriffe, and he liked the passengers, noting the strong features of the French colonial officials who were sent out under sealed orders, so that many of them did not know what port they would debark from until the last moment. Such official obedience Schweitzer regarded with awe. He was impressed, too, with an official who declaimed against the Mohamadan Negroes, saying they were lazy and unimaginative and contemptuous of all progress, but let a wandering priest of Islam on his ambling horse, with a yellow cloak over his shoulders, wander into a village, and the Negroes could not pay him enough tribute. In later years Schweitzer was to show that this early impression of Mohamadans had not changed: some of his tartest passages have been concerned with the "characteristic primitivism" of the Islamic religion.

Dakar disturbed him, but it was neither the heat nor the ugliness of the port which wrung his withers. For the first time he saw Africans maltreating donkeys. Two Negroes were sitting on a woodcart and thwacking at the donkey trying to make its way up a steep hill. Schweitzer ordered the Negroes off the cart and made them push it, offering his own strong shoulders to help relieve the burden. A French lieutenant who was satisfied to watch the scene commented:

"You'd better not go to Africa at all unless you can bear to see animals maltreated." Privately, Schweitzer told himself this might be one further reason for going to Africa.

At Konakri, on the Guinea Coast, he was amazed to discover that magnificent green woodlands flourished at the water's edge. He had studied innumerable natural sciences, but forgotten geography: he still retained a curious picture of Africa as a place where all the coastline was sandy desert. Through a telescope he saw the pointed huts of Negro villages—the first Negro houses he had ever seen.

For the rest of the journey the *Europe* passed close to the shore. It was a tragic shore. One after another appeared the Pepper Coast, the Ivory Coast, the Gold Coast, the Slave Coast. He fell to brooding over the unnumbered tragedies which had occurred deep in the forests beyond the thin shore-line. There were the green seas and the sand-bars throwing up their clouds of spray, and beyond these lay the endless dark land where the Europeans, the inheritors, held sway, every one of them implicated in the tragic drama, all of them coming as lords over the destinies of the Africans. The beauty of the coast surprised him. There were gaily colored flying fish, and snub-nosed sharks came close to the ship, and jelly-fish could be seen springing up in the phosphorescent foam "like glowing balls of metal." Never had he known such pleasure over a beautiful landscape mingled with such dread. And the landscape was more beautiful still when, beyond Cape Lopez, they transferred to a river-steamer at the mouth of the mighty Ogowe river. Nine years later he remembered vividly his exaltation as he journeyed down the Ogowe for the first time:

River and primeval forest. . . . Who can ever describe their first impression on our senses? We seemed to be dreaming. An ancient landscape, which elsewhere had seemed but the creation of man's fancy, had suddenly sprung to life. Impossible to say where the river ends and the land begins. A vast tangle of roots clothed in lianas rose from the water. Palm shrubs and palm trees, and among them other trees with green boughs and powerful branches and leaves, and standing among them trees towering heavenward, and vast fields of papyrus as high as a man with great fan-shaped leaves, and in all this lush greenness dead giants with decayed branches pointing high in the sky. Every gap in the forest revealed a blinding mirror of water, and with every bend of the river another branch of the river came in sight. A heron flies up heavily, only to settle on a dead stump. Tiny blue birds are skimming over the water, and high above us a pair of ospreys are circling. Then—over there—however improbable—two monkey tails are swinging from a palm tree. And then suddenly we see the owners of the tails. We have arrived in Africa! [1]

He had of course seen this strange landscape before; for it had been admirably depicted in one of the paintings of Grünewald, which reposed in the Colmar Museum. "An ancient landscape, which elsewhere had seemed but the creation of man's fancy . . ." But it was there in front of him, oily and yellow, strangely sinister, with its submerged sandbanks and tree-trunks floating just below the surface, always the forest, always the same yellow water. A Negro pilot stood at the wheel, and it was beyond Schweitzer's comprehension how anyone could navigate in this fantastic stream which was not a single river, but a whole river system, with innumerable branches each as wide as the Rhine.

[1] *On the Edge of the Primeval Forest.* By Albert Schweitzer. New York: The Macmillan Company. 1952.

They passed deserted villages. A trader muttered: "Fifteen years ago they were all flourishing." "Why not now?" Schweitzer asked. But the trader only shrugged his shoulders and whispered: "Alcohol." The steamer's paddle-wheels were driven by a wood-burning engine. At a small Negro village they came in sight of the stacked logs. A plank was thrown out from the bank, and the Negroes came on board, bearing the logs on their shoulders. Three thousand logs were brought onto the steamer, and paid for in alcohol. So they steamed up the ghostly river in the moonlight, while the stars shone on the water and the lightning flickered on the horizon, but they were still far from Lambaréné, two hundred and fifty miles from Cape Lopez.

At midnight they anchored in a sheltered bay, slipped under the mosquito curtains and tried to sleep. Before dawn the engines were throbbing again. It was another five hours before they reached Lambaréné. Then with difficulty the seventy packing cases were unloaded into dug-out canoes, and there was still a further journey to the mission station with the Negro rowers standing upright and singing as their long lean paddles sliced the water. The sun was sinking when they reached the mission station. He had thought to find a small settlement, but there was only a clearing in the dense forest, a few tumbledown buildings and some blue hills beyond.

The building set aside for Schweitzer and his wife was garlanded with flowers and palms in honor of his coming; some native children sang for him; a handful of white workers in the mission greeted him; but he was in a mood for rest, and soon he went off to the small four-roomed house on stilts where he would live. The bare walls were crumbling. Cockroaches and spiders were everywhere. Outside it was very dark, and the forest drums were throbbing. It was his second night in Africa, made memorable by a terrifyingly large spider which he squashed to death.

The filth, the spiders and the cockroaches were to haunt him to the end. There was never to be any peace from them. For the rest of his life in Africa there was to be constant war with them. There were other enemies. He was to discover that the worst enemy of all was inefficiency, not the deliberate inefficiency of the lazy, but the inefficiency which is endemic under the African sun. In that heat, in those forests, it needed a superhuman will to show any efficiency at all.

The Paris Mission had promised to have a small corrugated iron hospital ready for him. It was not there. The only available building which could be used as a makeshift hospital was a chicken-house nearby, the earth floor oily with refuse and the walls covered with a sickening froth of lichen. There was no roof. There were no windows. He borrowed a broom, swept the floor and whitewashed the walls, then installed some shelves and a camp-bed, which could be used as an operating table. On the shelves he laid out his medicines. The chicken-run became his consulting room, his surgery and dispensary.

From the first day patients came crowding to him. They came through the forests or in dug-out canoes, suffering from malaria, dysentery, framboesia, sleeping sickness, leprosy, ulcers, hernias, elephantiasis. An astonishing number suffered from hernia, which had to be operated on at once. The variety of their illnesses frightened and appalled him.

There were more patients than he could cope with. He was at a serious disadvantage in not having an interpreter—the interpreter who had been recommended to him and who had promised to be available was at this moment attending to a lawsuit in a distant town. There were even more serious disadvantages. The chicken-run hospital was an outrage. It was necessary to build a bigger one. During the summer, when it rains rarely, he could stand outside the chicken-run and attend to his patients in the open air, but when the rains came, he would need a reasonably strong building. By November he had built a hospital ward with corrugated iron walls and roof: large windows, concrete floor, shelves, wooden shutters. By December he had a waiting-room and a shed for the in-patients large enough to house 16 patients. Soon he was building a hut for sleeping sickness patients on the further side of the river. All through that year the building went on. In the first nine months he treated nearly 2,000 patients.

Schweitzer was accustomed to hard work, but this was the hardest he had known. His chief helpers were his wife, who prepared bandages and administered anaesthetics and saw that the surgical instruments were kept in good shape, and otherwise superintended the work in the wards. "First assistant to the doctor in Lambaréné" was the amazing Joseph Azoawami, who came as a patient and stayed on as a guide, spiritual counsellor to the sick and aide-de-camp. He had been a cook and knew something of anatomy, and though illiterate he possessed a phenomenal memory and could remember the shapes of the writing on the medicine bottles, so that in time he knew exactly what medicine to give his patients. He spoke French and English reasonably well, and knew eight African dialects. He was a tower of strength. He gave advice freely, and it was nearly always excellent. He suggested that Schweitzer should have nothing to do with patients on the verge of death; if they died, he would be held responsible. This was advice which Schweitzer could not accept in principle, though very often he was compelled to accept it in practice.

There were always emergency operations. A man suffering from strangulated hernia, his intestines blown up with gases, would come to the hospital weakened by a long and exhausting journey. He would be taken to the operating theatre. Mme. Schweitzer prepared the cone of ether and Joseph stood by, proud of his long rubber gloves and ready for any emergency.

The heat was terrible: the heat, the stench, the flies, the mosquitoes. Sunrise brought the tsetse fly, the night brought the mosquitoes. The ravages of the tsetse fly, which causes sleeping sickness, were spread all over central Africa. More than any other disease it had the effect of wasting the strength of the natives, killing them by slow degrees: first with unbearable headaches, then with drowsiness, finally with a coma that ends in death. To cure the disease, it was necessary to detect it in the early stages by means of a blood-examination, which was always time-consuming, because the thin, pale trypanosomes were so difficult to find under the microscope. Schweitzer would spend whole mornings hovering over his microscope, hoping to find some trace of the parasite, not daring to announce that the patient was free of sleeping sickness even if he failed to find it. He would take ten cubic centimetres of blood from a vein in the arm, place the blood in a centrifuge and remove the outer rings of blood from time to time. Every blood analysis except the last might be negative, or even the last might be negative, and still the doctor would have to search for the parasite. Sleeping sickness put a doctor on his mettle. It was not one disease but many, for invariably the patients suffered from rheumatism or pneumonia as well. And often Schweitzer had to ask himself whether it was right for him to spend whole mornings over the microscpe, when he should be dealing with the patients in the waiting-room, pulling their teeth or renewing their surgical dressings. The impatience of the sick is not a pleasant thing, and he admitted afterwards that he was sometimes so confused and nervous that he hardly knew where he was or what he was doing.

There were times when the strain was almost intolerable, when the heat, the stench, the raw wounds, the violent inflammations and the ugly fungus-like growths on the human body depressed him beyond measure. To see a dying baby, infected from its mother's breast with the raspberry-colored pustules of framboesia, was not conducive to a quiet demeanor. Patients came to him suffering from tropical sores which had eaten away all the flesh of their legs, so that the bones shone through like white islands. The pain was fearful, the smell was nauseating, and often enough there was little he could do except put the patient away in the isolation ward, where food would be brought to him; then in the utmost anguish the patient simply wasted away. Even when these sores could be cured, there was so much pain involved that it was almost preferable to let the patient die. To heal these sores, he had to put the patient under an anaesthetic and scrape carefully down to healthy tissue, while the blood flowed in streams. There would be careful applications of potassium permanganate, but almost every day the wound had to be inspected closely to see whether there were any new centres of infection. Sometimes many months passed before the patient was able to walk to the dugout canoe which would take him home.

Swamp-fever, tropical malaria, crawcraw, amoebic dysentery, hernias—these were the companions of his days and nights. He had steeled himself against death, but not against pain. "Pain," he wrote, "is a more terrible lord of mankind than even death itself." So when he saw death approaching he was curiously calm, but he could never shake himself free of his sensitivity to the pain of others. For consolation he would go to the lead-lined piano presented to him by the Bach Society of Paris and lose himself idly in practicing. And one day when he was particularly melancholy, and found himself playing one of Bach's organ fugues, it occurred to him that no harm would be done if he practiced seriously. He needed the stimulus of music. He worked better after playing seriously. In Strasbourg, after a long day spent in the Medical School, he had turned with relief to the organ, and with Ernst Münch at his side he had played strenuously for an hour, for two hours, before returning to his studies. Now, quite suddenly, he decided to study compositions by Bach, Mendelssohn, Widor, César Franck and Max Reger until he had learned every detail. If necessary, he would spend several months studying a single piece.

He had vowed himself to silence. In a sense he was breaking the vow; he was like a Trappist monk who suddenly breaks out into song. But his conscience was clear. Without music, his mind was in danger of breaking under the strain. With music performed strenuously, he could face the most fearful and delicate surgical operations with a quiet mind.

In Paris he had vowed to be "silent like a carp." But this vow too was lifted from him, when he presented himself at a mission conference at Samkita thirty miles up river and because he made no attempt to foist his theological views upon his brother missionaries, he was invited to take part in preaching, and was even permitted to share in the examination of the candidates for baptism. He gloried in his newfound freedom. But he preached only briefly and humbly, using the simplest words. When he was asked to express his opinion on a theological matter, a native preacher smiled condescendingly and pointed out that the matter was outside the doctor's province "because he is not a theologian, as we are."

He had started with a chicken-run. Now there were five substantial buildings belonging to the hospital, and there were plans for more buildings. Already the hospital was beginning to resemble a small village. He was in the position of a man who has to lay down the laws and proclaim the rights and duties of the villagers. They had the right to be cured of their diseases. In return they were asked to pay in bananas and manioc and labor for the doctor's services. There were also some elementary rules to be followed. These were read out six times a day in the dialects of the Galoas and the Pahuins, so that there should be no misunderstanding.

The Doctor's Standing Orders

1. Spitting near the doctor's house is strictly forbidden.
2. Those who are waiting must not talk to each other loudly.
3. Patients and their friends must bring with them food enough for one day, as they cannot all be treated early in the day.
4. Anyone who spends the night on the station without the doctor's permission will be sent away without any medicine.
5. All bottles and tin boxes in which medicines are given must be returned.
6. In the middle of the month, when the steamer has gone up the river, none but urgent cases may be seen till the steamer has gone down again, as the doctor is then writing to Europe to get more of his valuable medicines.[1]

Nothing that Schweitzer wrote later about those early days at Lambaréné was quite so revealing as the Standing Orders, which were read out very carefully and answered with a nodding of the head signifying that they were understood. At the end there was a coda, which carried a curious religious flavor: "And may the doctor's words be known in all the villages, both in the villages and on the lakes." It was as though the Standing Orders concluded with a statement which was at once an admonition and a blessing *urbi et orbi*.

These Standing Orders were necessary, and were to be added to from time to time. In the early days, when the equipment was still primitive, the village was ruled by a patriarch who seemed himself to have stepped out of a primitive age. The Alsatian peasant was close to the earth,

---

[1] *On the Edge of the Primeval Forest.* By Albert Schweitzer. New York: The Macmillan Company. 1952.

as the natives were, and some element of animism had clung to him through the years, unspoiled by theological meditations. He was complex and uncomplicated. One part of his capacious mind examined the natives from the high eminence of European culture; another part was examining them from inside. He was living close to them and probing into their physical bodies and being splattered by their blood. Gradually by a process of osmosis, he was being able to penetrate into their fetish-ridden minds and to feel a growing sense of intimacy with them. Occasionally there would be sparks of authoritarian temper, but in the early days these were rare. Through all his accounts of the first long visit to Lambaréné we are aware of a grave tenderness. He is telling about a successful operation on a native patient who had come to the hospital moaning with pain:

The operation is finished, and in the scarcely lighted dormitory I watch for the sick man's awaking. Scarcely has he recovered consciousness when he stares about him and cries again and again: "I've no more pain! I've no more pain!" His hand feels for mine and will not let it go. Then I begin to tell him and the others who are in the room that it is the Lord Jesus who sent the doctor and his wife to the Ogowe, and that white people in Europe gave them the money to live here and cure the sick Negroes. Then I have to answer questions as to who these white people are, where they live, and how they know the natives suffer so much from sickness. The African sun is shining through the coffee bushes into the dark shed, but we, black and white, sit side by side and feel that we know by experience the meaning of the words: "And all ye are brethren" (Matt. xxiii, 8).[2]

[2] *On the Edge of the Primeval Forest*. By Albert Schweitzer. New York: The Macmillan Company. 1952.

The same tenderness, and the same art in telling the story, occurs in an account of a woman suffering from mental illness:

It was my first contact with a mentally-diseased patient. It happened at night. I was knocked up and taken to a palm-tree where an elderly woman was bound with ropes. Around the fire in front of her sat all her family; behind them was the great wall of the forest which was jet-black. It was a glorious African night and the shimmering glow of the stars lit the scene. I ordered them to set her free, which they did, but with timidity and hesitation. The woman was no sooner free than she sprang at me in order to seize my lamp and throw it away. The natives fled shrieking in every direction and would not come any nearer, even when the woman, whose hand I had seized, sank quietly to the ground as I told her, and offered me her arm for an injection of morphia and scopolamin. A few moments later she followed me to a hut where in a short time she fell asleep.[3]

It was a time of growth, of new experiences, of blinding glimpses into the African soul. Fresh from Europe, he saw sometimes with startling clarity how fear could be transformed into love. Every morning he felt it an inexpressible mercy to be able to serve his brethren. Whenever he was exhausted by his labors in the surgery, he had only to remind himself that he was privileged beyond his deserts. His happiest writings from Africa date from those early years.

Often the new experiences were bewildering. One night, with the moon shining silver on the river, the dark forest brooding in the background, he found himself staring at the huge heads of two hippos rising above the surface. He ate

[3] *Ibid.*, p. 32.

monkey meat without relishing it and with no desire to shoot
monkeys to fill the pot; if you shot them when they were
swinging on the trees, as likely as not they would fall into
the undergrowth, and if you waded out among the swamps
and the thick grasses, you would probably find a baby monkey clinging to its dead mother. He kept a gun, but only to
shoot snakes and the eagles which plundered the nests of
of the weaver birds in the palms just outside his house. In
the hospital he was always being faced with improbable
complaints: the last thing he ever expected to see was a
native of the Ogowe suffering from nicotine poisoning. In
fact, hundreds of natives suffered from it. Tobacco, which
served as a form of currency, was imported into Equatorial
Africa in great leaves, and the natives were always smoking
their pipes. Diseases he had expected to find were notable
by their absence; until very recently he found no cases of
cancer or appendicitis.

All the time he was having to think profoundly about the
problem of the African in relation to the white man.

The problem was always there, and there were no easy
solutions. The colonizing power demanded tribute in the
form of taxes. In order to pay the taxes, the native had to
work in a way which would provide him with money to pay
the taxes. Every native above the age of fourteen had to pay
a poll tax of five francs a year, with the result that a man
with two wives and seven children was forced to pay fifty
francs a year. Further, the traders were committed to exacting *their* tribute in the form of money to be exchanged for
the inessentials which they displayed temptingly in their
stores—alcohol, razor-blades, chemises trimmed with lace,

openwork stockings, musical boxes and phonographs. As Schweitzer saw it, the state and commerce were in an unholy alliance to create in the native as many needs as possible. The colonizers therefore were behaving in a way which demonstrated that the interests of civilization and of colonization were opposed.

The true civilizer would come to the natives and offer them all that was best in European culture: he would give them schools, a network of medical facilities, he would teach them to lay out plantations and build houses of brick instead of bamboo. In Zululand, where agriculture and cattle-raising were possible, the civilizers were able to develop a native peasantry attached to their land and practicing home industries, but nothing comparable to this could be attempted in the great forests of the Ogowe, with their rich fields of mahogany, rosewood and coral-wood. Here was wealth to be plundered. One hundred fifty thousand tons of wood were exported from Cape Lopez in the year 1914. The whole economy of Gabon was founded on timber. If the market for timber collapsed, what then? Had the government and the merchants thought out their responsibility towards the native labor force? Obviously they had not. Schweitzer raged against the traders who imported *bric-à brac* to sell to the natives, but he could hardly blame them: the fault lay deeper—in the very nature of colonization itself, and in geography, and in history. At the heart of the problem lay the irresponsibility of the colonizers, themselves the products of geography and history. Their crime was that they came to Africa without assuming the burden of the responsibility which western civilization demanded they should assume. They came for loot. It never occurred to them to come for any other purpose.

When Schweitzer speaks of the responsibilities of western civilization in Africa, he speaks gravely and passionately. He saw all round him the consequences of western penetration. There were diseases natives suffered from only because they had been brought in contact with white men. There was the long, sordid history of slave-traffic on the coast. Along the Ogowe the natives were held in an economic stranglehold, for it was to the advantage of the white men to see that the timber trade flourished; but the timber trade was poison to the black man. "Whenever the timber trade is good," Schweitzer wrote, "permanent famine reigns in the Ogowe region." And he went on to explain that the natives who felled the forests had to live on imported rice and imported preserved food, which they purchased with the proceeds of their labor. Home industry became impossible when all the available labor force was sent to work in the forests. When the war came and it was no longer possible to export timber, the disastrous consequences of reliance on a single economy became only too apparent.

The longer he stayed in Africa, and the more he studied the behavior of the Negroes, the more intolerant he became of those who denied their virtues. Graceful and handsome, they walked the earth like men devoted to freedom. There were times when their quiet dignity shamed him. There was always the lean and handsome Joseph to demonstrate they could take to complicated skills and prove themselves the equals of Europeans. And he remembered that without Joseph's aid the hospital might easily have foundered in those early days, when there were hardly enough medicines in the medicine-chests and little enough equipment to serve the streams of natives who came to the hospital.

People wrote from Europe to ask him quite seriously whether any African could possibly understand the high morality of the Christian religion. He answered that they understood morality with the same instinctive grace as the best Christians, and he was always being startled by their natural ability to understand religion. Doctrine puzzled them, and they were totally incapable of understanding Christianity as a continuing historical process. They saw Christianity as something that existed outside time; they saw in flashes, with wonderful clarity.

The educated natives genuinely astonished him by their skills. Government-trained natives drew up complicated documents faultlessly; they could draw up pages of complex statistics without mistakes. Once when a native government clerk came to the hospital, Schweitzer saw some of his essays. A missionary was staying at the hospital. When the clerk left, Schweitzer and the missionary exchanged glances and agreed that neither could compete with the native in essay writing. Schweitzer, who had written many essays, and often with angelic power and grace, was not being ironic.

Quite early in his stay in Africa Schweitzer became aware of the prodigious intelligence which lurks in the African mind. Potentially, the intelligence of the African was in no way inferior to the intelligence of the white man. The tragedy was that the intelligent native, uprooted from his village and working among white men, lived the life of the dissatisfied outcast and was a prey to the traders who encouraged his love for gaudy clothes and trinkets. "We Negro intellectuals are in a very uncomfortable position," an educated native said. "Our women are too uneducated to make good wives for us. They should import wives for us from the higher tribes in Madagascar." Schweitzer relates the story with considerable sympathy for the Negro.

His sympathies however were not always with the natives. When they were patients in the hospital, he brooded over their sufferings, amazed by their calm endurance and their gentleness to one another. When he employed them as laborers, they often enraged him. Heat and worry and the constant battle for supplies made him impatient and nervous. Because they were feckless and often disobedient, and had no particular liking for work, he found himself shouting at them. Once a native had the temerity to answer back. "Doctor, don't shout at us! It's your own fault! If you will stay with us, then we'll work! If you go back to the hospital and stay with the sick patients, we are alone and do nothing!" Schweitzer recognized the truth of the complaint. He decided he would have to spend time from the hospital and oversee their work. Characteristically, he decided to make them sweat for his pains. "So I made them work," he wrote later, "till their dark skins glistened with sweat, and succeeded in getting a certain amount of work out of them."

The natives had a wonderful faculty for losing tools and simply forgetting the job they had been ordered to do. They tried his patience so much that he complained wearily: "It is so hard to remain humane and to continue to be the standard-bearer of civilization." In later years—especially in a collection of stories collected together under the title

African Notebook—he poked fun cruelly at their laziness, their shiftlessness, their continual stealing, but he was careful to add that though undisciplined and unreliable, they were essentially noble and well-bred in their manners, gentle and kind-hearted, possessed of amazing fortitude and loyalty, working calmly and competently even after they had suffered intolerable abuse. He found them lacking in that direct sympathy for their fellowmen which Christianity encourages and says categorically that they are concerned with themselves alone, only to disprove the statement a few lines later by telling stories of how they risked their lives to save white men who had given them repeated tongue-lashings. "Really to understand the African," he writes, "one must get to know him man to man." In that simple statement he may have laid the foundations for one of the great revolutions of our time.

Most of all Schweitzer was attracted by the picture of the African as "a child of freedom." He found Rousseau's "noble savage" close to the truth. As he watched them arriving in their dugouts and climbing the sandy shore to the hospital, suffering the hideous ravages of tropical disease, with suppurating wounds and strange yellow and purple growths exuding from their bodies he saw eloquence in their gestures and nobility in their bearing. They lived (when it was possible) in the utmost freedom, and died quietly. They did not fear death, and lacked the European's horror of it. He says at one point that they are completely lacking in a sense of social life, and elsewhere he finds himself approving a social organization by which no widows are left unprovided for and no orphans are neglected. As we read Schweit-

zer on the subject of the African, we see him speaking from
different vantage-points. Sometime he speaks from the
heights of dogmatic Christian morality; a cold light shines
in his eyes; who are these children of innocence to set themselves up against me? But these moments are rare. Impatience and ill-temper are forgotten in the surgery and the
wards. At such times he writes about them without cruelty
and with astonishing tenderness, "man to man." Once, in
an effort to explain to himself why the Negro took with such
difficulty to working for a white employer, he wrote: "The
Negro is not idle: he is a free man." At another time he
said: "I can no longer talk ingenuously about the laziness
of the Negro after seeing fifteen of them spending thirty-six
hours uninterruptedly rowing, to bring me a white man who
was seriously ill."

Again and again Schweitzer hints that there must be some
kind of compact between the Negro and the white man.
They face one another across vast barriers of time and
history. And sometimes he would say that only Christianity
could dissolve those barriers. For himself, he destroyed the
barriers in the operating theatre, and he was a little surprised
to see them rising again once he was outside the hospital.
From the beginning he insisted upon segregation. In a
phrase which reveals much of his own strength and some of
his weakness, he said: "Admitted I am their brother, but it
must be clearly understood I am the elder brother." In his
case the statement was justified, but few white men possessed his moral authority; and the native with his unerring
intuition is only too adept in detecting the moral faults of a
white man:

Where the native finds goodness, justice and genuineness of character, real worth and dignity behind the external dignity given him by social circumstances, then he bows and acknowledges his master. When he fails to find them, then he remains defiant even when he gives the impression of submission, and he says to himself: "This white man is no more of a man than I am, for he is no better than I am." [4]

All through those early days in Africa Schweitzer was attempting to define the relationship between the black man and the white. He did not always succeed. It was not only that his own anaemia and hot temper got in the way, but the African seemed often strange to him, one moment a brother, the next receding into the dark tides of the forest and becoming indistinguishable from the shadows. Half of Schweitzer's mind was still in Europe. He would take refuge from the oppressive heat and the oppressive presence of the Negroes by playing Bach; and standing there, amid the intense bright lights at the summit of the western tradition, he could with difficulty reconcile himself to these sturdy savages, who lived for the moment and possessed no known history. By charity and doggedness and love he won their hearts, but they could never entirely win his. As he recounts his life among the natives, he sometimes gives the impression of playing on them as if they were some strange musical instrument. He plays it quietly, pouring his affection into it. Suddenly there is a jangling chord. He pauses, startled, and continues playing until another jangling chord disturbs his equanimity. Though he knew their physical bodies, there were regions of the African soul he never dared to plumb.

[4] *On the Edge of the Primeval Forest.* By Albert Schweitzer. New York: The Macmillan Company. 1952.

So there passed fourteen months of gruelling work under
the hot sun. The heavy rains of winter had gone, and it was
summer again, the wet choking summer when there is no
wind and the heat at noon is hardly distinguishable from the
heat at midnight. That first year he had worked to the uttermost, slept little, poured out affection boundlessly, and now
at last his strong body was showing signs of weariness and
strain. Tropical anaemia had made inroads in his strength,
and he was suffering from a large abscess. He needed a rest.
However much he wanted to stay, he knew it would be dangerous, and so he made arrangements to consult the military
doctor at Cape Lopez, abandoning the hospital for a little
while to Joseph.

He had scarcely reached the coast when the abscess burst.
The doctor ordered complete rest. So he sat with his wife on
a verandah overlooking the sea, amazed beyond measure
because there were sea-winds blowing on his face. At Lambaréné the only winds that ever touched him came when the
tornadoes came crashing through the forests in the rainy
season. Characteristically, he employed his enforced leisure
to write a lengthy account of the timber trade on the Ogowe.

At the end of July 1914 he left Cape Lopez by river-
steamer for Lambaréné and profited by the long journey to
write a consecutive account of the social problems in the
forests of the Ogowe. The patients were waiting for him and
he observed with satisfaction that Joseph had accomplished
his task well: the hospital was in good shape.

He had almost forgotten the war clouds which hovered
over Europe. He read newspapers rarely, for here, where
time stood still, the brief and passing events which filled

newspapers seemed meaningless in comparison with the huge forest and vast river which shadowed their lives. He spent the two days after his return working feverishly; patients who had been sent away when he left were clamoring to come in. On the third day he sent Joseph with a message to the captain of the river steamer—it was a question of some medicines to be taken to a patient on the coast. When Joseph returned, Schweitzer knew by the expression of his face that the thing he had dreaded had happened. A message from the ship's captain said: "Europe is at war."

That same afternoon a river-boat came to the landing-stage, full of native soldiers armed with carbines. They marched up to the hospital, bearing an order of arrest. As enemy aliens, Dr. and Mme. Schweitzer were ordered to place themselves in the custody of the armed Africans and to have no more contact with their patients or with the Frenchmen in the neighboring mission. It seemed that out of nowhere a black shutter had fallen over all his work in Africa.

~~~ *6* ~~

The Ruined Years

WHEN THE ARMED AFRICANS
forced their way into the hospital compound on that August
afternoon, Schweitzer knew that the venture to which he had
dedicated his life had lost its meaning. He had regarded
himself as a missionary from enlightened Europe to darkest
Africa; now the darkness was descending over Europe, and
there was nowhere to turn. Years were to pass before he felt
strong enough, or dedicated enough, to resume his work in
Africa with a full heart. The shutter had fallen. For nearly
ten years he was to be a prisoner or a wanderer, a plague to
doubts, so unsure of himself that it sometimes seemed to
him that all his preparations for a life spent in Africa were
vain: better never to have come to Africa at all than to
watch the darkness of Europe falling over Lambaréné.

The order from Brazzaville placing him in solitary con-
finement meant an end to the hospital: the patients were
sent home: silence reigned. In that small teeming city he had
built there was no one now except Joseph, who wandered
about like a ghost, asking strange questions about a strange
war, standing guard over the boxes of medicaments and

bandages, while Schweitzer trembled in the house on the hill, thinking about Alsace overrun with German soldiers already on the march towards France. He had no hope that it would be a short war, no belief that the war would solve any problems. It was as though on the body of the world a violent and incurable inflammation had broken out, an inflammation so virulent that the world might die of it.

At first, when the hospital was closed down, he had thought of spending the days of his imprisonment resting quietly: he was still suffering from the abscess: his strength was exhausted despite the brief holiday on the coast. But he was incapable of resting for long, and that same evening he found himself taking up the pages of a long forgotten manuscript on the mysticism of St. Paul. He worked on it for a few days, then gave it up. St. Paul was a subject to be studied in a quieter mood; and his mind going back to the long debates he had enjoyed in Berlin at the turn of the century in the circle of the brilliant Ernst Curtius, he remembered a phrase overheard in a debate—*Wir Epigonen*, "We, the Inheritors." From there he went on to ponder the history of the philosophy of civilization he had once thought to write, and now he decided to write an account of the inheritors who had so unwisely misspent their inheritance. He chose the title: *The Decay and Restoration of Civilization.* In a sense it would be a clinical treatise, with the diagnosis of the disease followed by the cure. But as he began to write, he was not at all sure the patient would ever be cured. Western civilization was bleeding to death.

It was not a passing mood. The war cut him to the quick, and he was never able to conceal its ravages from himself, though he did his best to prevent the native house-servants from being contaminated. When illustrated magazines arrived, he hid them from the Africans, afraid they would learn too much from the grim pictures and the grimmer texts. With horror went a sense of shame and guilt, inextinguishable, made all the greater by his loneliness and his profound knowledge of the split in the European soul.

The war frightened and puzzled the Africans. Prices rose sharply: tobacco, sugar, rice and kerosene were soon almost unobtainable. Before the end of the year ten Frenchmen had left the neighborhood of Lambaréné to be killed in France. When the news was brought to a Pahuin chieftain, he asked: "Why don't the tribes meet for a palaver? How can they pay for all these dead men?" It was not easy to explain to the Pahuins why the whites, who brought the Gospel of Love to Africa, were killing one another and tossing to the winds the Sermon on the Mount. Schweitzer did not attempt to explain the war to them. All he would tell them was that "something frightful" had happened, something almost beyond the control of human forces and perhaps almost beyond the control of God.

The war affected the entire economy of Gabon. Because so few ships called at Port-Gentil, export of timber came to an end. Usually the forest trees were felled during the dry season, between June and October. The indentured lumbermen found themselves jobless, with little money to take home and no way of reaching their villages along the Loango coast except by walking, for there were no more river boats. Poverty stalked French Africa. Once when

Joseph complained about the growing poverty, Schweitzer heard himself saying: "There are more important things than a rise in prices. Ourselves, we think about the groans of the wounded and the death rattles of the dying." Joseph looked up in astonishment, and Schweitzer remembered afterwards that he bore an expression which suggested a sudden revelation.

Characteristically, the French authorities began to circumvent their own orders. The hospital was closed down and the gates sealed, but sickness remained—no orders by the district commandant could put an end to it. One day a messenger arrived from the district commandant's office, bearing a message so out of character with all the previous messages Schweitzer had received that for a while he was nonplussed; then he saw that the messenger was ailing. He knew then why the meaningless message had been delivered. In effect he had received a discreet order from the administration to reopen the hospital unofficially, but only for such patients as the administration wanted him to heal.

It was a half-hearted solution to the difficulty, and as usual Schweitzer had little patience with official sleight of hand. Soon after he was interned, he had written to Charles Widor and other members of the Bach Society of Paris, begging them to use their influence to let the hospital continue. Now at last at the end of November, while the rains whistled in the palm trees and the earth was so waterlogged that the foundations of the hospital were in danger of crumbling away, there came an order signed by the Resident-General of the Gabon urging him to reopen the hospital and to continue exactly as he had done before the outbreak of

war. For four months he had lived under house arrest. Now
he was free to go about his affairs as he pleased, and he
threw himself into the work of healing the natives, though
the last of the gold francs in his strongbox were nearly gone
and supplies of food and drugs were dangerously low and
there was almost no one to assist him. Worse still, he had to
contend with the famine which began to spread over the
land, the result of the depredations of hordes of elephants.
Twenty elephants had been known to trample down a whole
plantation in a single night. All through that winter and
spring this little corner of French Equatorial Africa was
caught in the grip of a relentless misery. The rains fell; the
war went on; and every day there were new patients arriving
at the hospital, while the doctor watched and wondered how
far he could stretch his supplies.

When summer came he was still at work, and close to
exhaustion. As usual he was spending the nights on the book
and the days in hospital rounds. He was trying to work out
the basis for his book on civilization. "How," he asked himself, "could there be brought about a marriage between the
rigorous, affirmative western spirit and the simple goodness
of Christianity?" He did not know the answers, but he knew
that an answer must be found. Pondering the problem, he
was like someone leaning with all his strength on an iron
door that refused to yield.

The door yielded one evening when he least expected it.
In September 1915 he happened to be staying with his wife
at Cape Lopez when he received an urgent summons to attend the ailing wife of a missionary at N'Gomo, 160 miles
upstream. The only available ship was a small steamer, tow-

ing an overladen barge. There were no white men on board. The Africans let him share their cooking-pot. He sat on deck, scribbling industriously, trying to get to the heart of the problem. On the third day at sunset, while the river-steamer was pushing its way through a herd of hippopotamus, there flashed through his mind the unexpected and unhoped-for words: *"Ehrfurcht vor dem Leben."*

Ehrfurcht means more than "reverence." It has overtones of awe and shuddering wonder and great blessedness. Before God a man may abase himself in holy awe. A man may humble himself before the infinite spaces of the firmament. So should a man humble himself before the ever-present miracle of life. Let him regard that miracle with reverential fear and wonder, and let him never cease regarding it in this way, for all life is the vehicle of the power of God.

But in that mysterious word *Ehrfurcht* there are still further overtones: a sense of the soul perfecting itself and of developing values. The fear, the wonder are not things in themselves, but are to be used for the divine purpose of perfection; and all living things are magnified by the awe with which they are beheld. There is a sense in which *Ehrfurcht* is as elemental as the shuddering delight of Adam as he opened his eyes on the first morning of the world. There is another sense in which *Ehrfurcht* reaches beyond the contemplative into pity for all suffering things, a pity so deep that man is compelled to change the world even while glorifying it, for at the heart of the mystery lies the tragedy which Schweitzer stated most succinctly when he said: "The world is a ghastly drama of will-to-live divided against itself." Every act of affirmation is potentially deathly: the roots of

a young tree may strangle the roots of another. So, in
Schweitzer's words: "One will-to-live merely exerts its will
against the other, and has no knowledge of it." Yet man,
endowed with thought and a holy spirit, may act as a kind
of moderator: his task is simply to celebrate God by his
devotions, and not the least of his devotions are those acts
intended to spare pain. Pity and love purify the will-to-live,
and every wound that is healed partakes of blessedness. A
man who possesses an entire veneration and awe of life will
not simply say his prayers: he will throw himself into the
battle to preserve life, if for no other reason than that he is
himself an extension of the life around him, life being so
holy and every man being part of this holiness. A man re-
joicing in that veneration for life is therefore led "into an
unrest such as the world does not know, but he obtains from
it a blessedness which the world cannot give." And if his
task is harder, because he assumes such huge responsibilities,
the rewards are greater, for those who help to preserve life
and heal wounds and diminish pain come to know the deep-
est happiness known to men.

Again and again, at different times of his life, Schweitzer
was to elaborate on this primitive and mysterious *Ehrfurcht*,
which is so much more than "reverence." It was a thing rid-
dled with paradoxes, but they seemed to be those final paradoxes which lie at the heart of the mystery, like the positive
and negative charges on electrons. Almost he seems to regard *Ehrfurcht* as an elemental passion sweeping through
all nature, and made conscious in man. It is not a gentle
thing. It can shake a man to his roots, and overwhelm him,
but at the very moment of being overwhelmed, he discovers

an unsuspected and surprising freedom from the world; for in these torments he overcomes the world. At last the will-to-live, that fierce affirmative force which holds us all by the throat, vanishes. In its place there is only the will-to-love, and the blessedness of healing, and the sense of communion with all living things.

On the river-steamer bound for N'Gomo, watching the herd of hippopotamus in the river, which seemed to seethe and swell as they splashed ferociously across, making a strange thudding sound, Schweitzer found four words which were to haunt him for the rest of his life. On these words he was to erect his philosophy. Henceforward he would demand of himself an intense devotion to the little flickering flame of life—every leaf, every insect, every animal was sacred. Sometimes it would be necessary to kill one kind of life in order that another should survive, and when this happened Schweitzer would find himself on the horns of an intolerable dilemma. He found life even in ice-crystals, and demanded that no one should break them. No grasses should be needlessly trodden on, no twigs should be needlessly bent. Because life was the supreme marvel it must be celebrated: the smallest of living things were as as valuable as the greatest. When a friend trod on a worm in Lambaréné, he was told: "You should apologize to him. After all you are a guest in his country." And when Schweitzer ate a grapefruit in the morning, he would drop some juice on the floor for the ants and watch them crowding round and say: "They are just like cattle coming to the pond."

Innumerable stories have been told of Schweitzer's affection for living things. Many of the stories seem whimsical, but Schweitzer himself was never more deadly serious than when he spoke of the little flame of life which courses through the frail bodies of moths and ants. Like the Jains in India, who wear masks over their mouths to prevent themselves from breathing in the small animalcules in the air, and who carefully brush the chairs they are going to sit on because some invisible living creature may be sitting there, he is inclined to regard the life in a single bacteria as important as the life of an animal. When he is forced to kill bacteria by the application of methyl violet on a wound, he is aware that he is committing a crime. He stands in judgment: a crime must be committted in order that a good shall prevail. All through life men must stand in judgment, weighing good against evil, continually committing crimes and therefore irremediably attached to evil. The words "reverence for life" conceal the tragic sense which underlies Schweitzer's concept of *Ehrfurcht vor dem Leben*. The English words also conceal the fact that the most important element in the word *Ehrfurcht* is *Furcht*, which means "fear." [1]

When Schweitzer first wrote these words, he was slowly awakening from the stupor which affected him during the first year of the war, that senseless war which seemed to contain within itself all the evil he was vowed to combat. At night, looking out on the dark coffee bushes and softly waving palms, he would gaze into the distance and see the war as though it were taking place before his eyes: a sick man

---

[1] The word *Ehrfurcht* does not appear in Luther's translation of the Bible. It seems to have been first used by Johann Geyler von Kaysersberg, who was born in Schweitzer's birthplace and in whose writings Schweitzer may have first set eyes on it.

contemplating the sickness of a continent. All that year he
was ill. Tropical anaemia had set in. The slightest exertion
tired him. Strength returned in the early fall of 1915, and
when the dry season came there was less work to do at the
hospital. With the rains came disease, misery and the
dreaded march of the traveler ants. About these particular
ants Schweitzer had decided opinions. Whenever he found
them, he killed them—mercilessly, brutally, by fire, by poison, by whatever lay at hand.

Traveler ants are terrifying. They march in columns, five
or six abreast, and destroy everything in their path. Once
Schweitzer watched such a column passing near his house
uninterruptedly for thirty-six hours. They marched in forma-
tion, flanked by warrior ants which turned outward on difficult terrain to protect the travelers in their midst; and sometimes they marched in long parallel columns separated by
immense distances. Nothing was safe from them. If the column climbed a tree, a spider trembling on the highest
branch would fall a prey to them; and if the spider flung
himself in despair to the ground, there were traveler ants
waiting for him. If they invaded a chicken run, they forced
themselves into the mouths and nostrils of the chickens and
tore them to pieces until only their white bones were left.
They came silently and unheralded, and they were not
afraid to attack men. Once in the winter of 1916, when
Schweitzer was staying at Cape Lopez, he saw a victim of
sleeping sickness lying in the sand, his sprawling body covered with ants. To protect himself the man had buried his
head in the sand. When Schweitzer came upon the man, it
was sunset and the blue sea lay in the golden light of the

setting sun. It might have been a scene of magical beauty, if it had not been for the naked man alive with ants.

The war dragged on. Few ships now called at Lambaréné. The poverty of the natives grew greater; many were being impressed, to become coolies in the Cameroons. The sight of these natives being taken off to a war which they would never understand alarmed Schweitzer. One day at N'Gomo, he stood on the river bank and watched a river steamer vanishing into the distance with its chain-gang of coolies, leaving a trail of smoke on the sky, and turned to see an old woman weeping for the son she might never see again. To comfort her, he took her hand, but she did not stop weeping. "And then," he said, "I felt suddenly that I was crying with her, silently, towards the setting sun, as she was."

The hospital continued, but only for a little while longer. In September 1917 the Clemenceau government issued a stringent decree against all enemy aliens within the French empire. They were to be rounded up and brought to internment camps in France. On the day when the decree reached the Gabon, the hospital came to an end. In front of him lay years of sickness and wandering. It was seven years before he came to Lambaréné again.

He was given orders to disband the hospital and collect his belongings for the journey in twenty-four hours. Fortunately the ship which was to take him back to France was delayed, and there was time to stow the drugs and medical instruments away in a corrugated iron shed. He dared not take with him his notes for the book on the decay of civilization, so he spent two nights making a short summary of the work in French and left the original manuscript in the hands of an American missionary, who detested philosophy and considered it would better to burn the notes rather than safeguard them. Schweitzer disguised his summary by inserting chapter-headings which somehow gave it the appearance of a history of the Renaissance. Two days before the ship sailed, he had to operate quickly on a strangulated hernia.

Life on the *Afrique*, which brought him with Mme. Schweitzer back to France, was a horror of boredom. As enemy aliens, they were under close guard and forbidden to talk to anyone except a steward especially assigned to watch over them. They were confined to their small cabin, and were allowed out for exercise only under strict supervision. Schweitzer said later that, since he was in no mood for writing, he spent his time in learning by heart some of the Bach fugues and Widor's Sixth Organ Symphony. The top of his trunk became an imaginary organ console and the feet pounded imaginary pedals on the floor. It was a game he had played many times in his youth, and it was to help him through all the months of imprisonment that followed.

At Bordeaux the Schweitzers were taken straight from the ship to the Caserne de Passage, one of those huge, cold and ill-lit buildings near the port which could be used as quarters for soldiers or as prisons simply by changing the guards. Here they remained through the bitter winter of 1917. Schweitzer grew ill with dysentery. He fought it off with emetin, but he was still weak when the spring came, and for years afterwards he suffered from the after-effects of that illness which struck him immediately on his return to France.

Then one day in the spring there came at a few hours'
notice orders to pack. Once again there was a terrible flurry
of activity as everyone attempted to put his small possessions
in order. It was night. A single candle illuminated the great
hall where the internees were busy with their crates and
duffel-bags. The gendarmes were furious, barked orders,
kept asking the internees why they didn't go about their
business quicker, and relented a little when they learned that
everyone thought the order was for the following night.
Then they were sent down to Garaison in the Pyrenees where
in a large monastery thousands of internees were camp-
ing out. The monastery, which had been abandoned at the
time of separation between the Church and the State,
housed enemy aliens from all over the world. Here were
Austrian shoemakers, white-robed missionaries from the
Sahara, men from South America and China who had been
taken prisoner on the high seas, artists, bank managers,
waiters, engineers, architects. There were Arabs, Greeks
and Turks accompanied by their veiled wives. There were
seamen from captured freighters. Schweitzer the doctor and
Schweitzer the psychologist looked at the motley crowd of
prisoners and decided that the horrors of Bordeaux were
over; with so much talent going to waste, he could at least
sit at their feet and learn from them. Garaison means "healing"; and in that crumbling monastery at the foot of the
snow-white Pyrenees, his health came back again.

The governor was a former colonial official and a theoso-
phist, kindly, gentle, unusually tolerant. He inaugurated
study circles, and did his best to mitigate the hardships of
internment. Though he was the only doctor there, Schweit-

zer was forbidden to attend the sick. Such were the rules, pronounced by the government in Paris. The governor decided to circumvent the rules. Dentists were allowed to practice; then why not doctors? The governor found some pretext for giving Schweitzer the same privileges as the dentists; a room was set apart for him; and there, after receiving patients all day, Schweitzer spent the evenings working on his philosophy of civilization. He wrote a long segment describing the Civilized State. The deliberate irony pleased him: during that terrible winter there was hardly a civilized state left on earth.

In Garaison Schweitzer learned a good deal which he was to put to use later. The camp contained scholars in all branches of learning. Schweitzer studied hard. He learned about banking, architecture, factory building, the growth of cereals, and how to build a furnace. It was a liberal education. The monastery at Garaison became a kind of international university, but not all the internees took part. The snow lay deep on the ground. The monastery was inadequately heated. Many simply became listless, wandering desultorily round and round the courtyard, waiting for the sound of the trumpet at dusk which would send them running back into the huge grey building, a prey to the disease of acedia. When it rained, they stood about apathetically in the long corridors. Schweitzer noted that imprisoned seamen knew how to pass the time—it was something they learned from their years at sea—but ordinary workmen condemned to idleness became grotesquely miserable. Musicians could play their instruments, but what of the man who had spent his days at a lathe? what of the cooks, who were no longer allowed to cook? For the first time Schweitzer was made aware of immense unsuspected areas of human experience and of the limitless wastes of boredom in prison-camps, though he was rarely bored.

Cooks and musicians had their own way of solving these problems. One day Schweitzer found himself accosted by a gypsy. The gypsy asked whether he was the Albert Schweitzer mentioned in Romain Rolland's *Musiciens d'aujourd'hui*. Schweitzer nodded. The gypsy, who was the leader of a group of musicians, was overjoyed and invited Schweitzer to attend the performances given in the loft. Also Schweitzer had the right to be serenaded, a right which was also granted to his wife. On the following Tuesday Mme. Schweitzer woke on her birthday serenaded by a gypsy orchestra playing *The Tales of Hoffmann*.

When the monastery kitchens failed to produce savory meals, amateur cooks from an abandoned prison camp asked to be allowed to take over. They promised they would be able to produce better meals and offered to accept dire punishment if they failed. They were tailors, hat-makers and basket-weavers: good solid men: and every dish they prepared was a triumph. They showed themselves so much better than the professionals that the professionals were thrown out of the kitchens. Schweitzer asked them how they were able to prepare vast quantities of food as delicately as if they were preparing small intimate meals. "One must know all kinds of things," he was told, "but the important thing is to cook with love and care." It was a lesson he had learned long ago in Africa.

At the end of March their wanderings began again. This

time they were sent to St. Rémy in Provence. Here the prisoners, many of them Alsatians, were housed in an asylum. The place seemed strangely familiar, and suddenly it dawned on Schweitzer that he had been there before and had gazed, as though in some past life, on those squat stoves and bellying flue-pipes which stretched across the whole length of the rooms, on those barren walls which had absorbed the cries of so many insane inmates in the past. Then he realized he was living in the asylum where Vincent van Gogh had spent his days. It was oddly disturbing, but he took consolation from the fact that he was standing where van Gogh had once stood.

Now once again, as in Garaison, he imposed order on his disordered life. Again he practiced medicine on the patients, again he played the organ by running his hands over an imaginary console, and at night he continued working on his study of civilization, and sometimes he was able to sit all day over the notes for the chapters on the Civilized State. But the fevers and the dysentery returned, and in the last weeks of his stay at St. Rémy he was violently ill. His wife sickened. He was almost too weak to move when he received news that there would be an exchange of prisoners. He was to be sent back to Alsace.

It was the middle of July 1918, with the war grinding toward its end. They were to return to Germany through Switzerland. At sunrise the internees were loaded into trucks and driven to Tarascon, where they had to wait in a freight shed half a mile away from the station. Heavily laden with luggage, they were then ordered to march along the rough shingle between the railroad lines. Schweitzer shouldered as

much luggage as he could, and he was walking with his wife
along the lines when a cripple he had treated at St. Rémy
came up to him. "Let me help you," the cripple said. "You
can see I am not carrying anything." Schweitzer was
touched, and gave the cripple a small burden to carry.
"Since that day," Schweitzer wrote later, "I have kept the
vow I made that I would always help people who are heavily laden in stations."

Early in the morning of July 15th the long train of exchanged prisoners reached Zurich. It was one of his griefs
that he had been forgotten by the world, as though he were
some object that "had fallen on the floor and lay hidden un-
derneath the wardrobe." In Zurich he received proof that
he was still vividly remembered, for when the train stopped
he heard the voices of old friends calling to him—there was
Arnold Meyer, the theologian, Robert Kaufmann, the singer,
and many others, who had heard by some mysterious means
that he was passing through Switzerland.

But the gaiety on the platform in Zurich was only fleeting:
soon the train was making its way to the German border.
He knew or guessed the misery which lay ahead, and stood
at the window, lapping up the clear and peaceful beauty of
Switzerland, the well-tended fields, the houses dancing in the
sun. Constance, just inside the German border, was a dark
city of emaciated men and women given over to despair.
Mme. Schweitzer was permitted to leave immediately for
her parents' home in Strasbourg, while her husband was
force to remain in Constance until formalities had been
completed. He reached Strasbourg later that night. The city
was blacked out. He found himself walking in the darkened

streets towards the familiar places where he had studied long ago, and that night he found refuge in a friend's house near St. Thomas's Church.

His greatest, his overwhelming desire was to return to Günsbach, which was in the fighting zone; it was some days before he received a permit to return home. At last he was allowed to take the train to Colmar. The little train to Günsbach was no longer running, and the last ten miles of the journey he did on foot.

He had bidden farewell to the Münster valley on Good Friday, 1913. Now he could hardly recognize it. The forests of pine and beech had been scorched off the hills. Everywhere he came upon brick emplacements for machine-guns and the rubble of shelled houses. As he strode through the villages which lie along the banks of the river Fecht, he saw posters urging everyone to wear their gas-masks and he heard the dull roar of cannon beyond the hills. Günsbach however, low down in a hollow between the hills, had survived almost intact, though the vines were shriveled and the corn had turned black in the hot summer and the potato crop was ruined. Everywhere there was desolation and heart-rending misery. With the fighting coming closer, the peasants knew they would be never be able to bring in the second crop of hay in the meadows. He stared at splintered tree stumps and listened to the bellowing of hungry cattle. But his father was alive and strong and the manse was untouched by gunfire; he could sleep in the room he had slept in when he was a child, before the dreams of Africa gripped him. When August came, the thunderheads rose in the sky, and instead of rain there were dust-storms, the earth all charred and worn, and in the heat, with the gunfire resounding off the hills, he knew he was beaten—beaten down as though a great shovel had leapt out of the sky to smash him against the hot earth.

He had fought off sickness and weariness until he came home to his village, but now tropical anaemia and dysentery fought within his exhausted body and left him helpless. He had high fever, and there were sudden outbreaks of torturing pain. At the end of August he made his way to Strasbourg, consulted doctors and learned that he would have to be operated on. A little while later, when he was recovering from the effects of the operation, he was offered medical charge of two small wards at a Strasbourg hospital. At the same time he was allowed to resume his duties as pastor of St. Nicholas's Church. Once again medicine and religion were being harnessed together. As his strength returned, he set about practicing the organ. And on his birthday, on January 14, 1919, Mme. Schweitzer gave him her most imaginative birthday present—a daughter he called Rhena in honor of the Rhine which flows through Alsace.

The wounds were healing, but still the weariness and the fret remained. He tried not to think of Africa; he was a curate and a physician, eking out a small living in the hospital wards. His manuscript on Bach's chorale preludes was in Lambaréné; so was the major part of his work on civilization; so were a hundred other scraps and outlines of books which would never be written. There was almost no hope that he would ever see Africa again.

Unknown to him there were people in England and

Sweden who remembered his work vividly and were looking
forward to the day when he would return to Africa. Suddenly, just before Christmas, 1919, when he was busy wrap-
ping Christmas parcels to be sent to friends in Germany,
there arrived a letter from the Archbishop of Canterbury
enclosing an invitation from Archbishop Nathan Soderblom,
urging him to deliver the Olaus-Petri lectures at the University of Upsala the following spring. He was a sick man,
weary of his dreams, appalled by the grinding misery of
Germany, and now help was coming from a quarter whence
he least expected it. Archbishop Soderblom was a famous
theologian and the head of the Protestant Church in Sweden;
he had read all of Schweitzer's books; and his invitation
promised an end to obscurity and poverty.

Schweitzer replied immediately, saying that he was grateful for the invitation and would be delighted to accept it.
There was some discussion about the subject of the lectures.
The university, through the Archbishop, requested, but did
not demand, the privilege of publishing the lectures. He was
invited to stay as long as he pleased in the Archbishop's palace and promised the best doctors in Sweden to aid him in
recovering his health.

In the late spring of 1920 the obscure curate from Strasbourg came to Sweden and gave a series of lectures on "The
Ethical Basis of Civilization." His last lecture was devoted
to the concept of *Ehrfurcht vor dem Leben* and he was so
deeply moved by the fierce enthusiasm of his audience that
there were long moments when he was tongue-tied, unable
to go on, gazing in despairing silence at the students as they
cheered wildly. He had come to Sweden tired, depressed, and

ailing. Under the care of Archbishop Nathan Soderblom
he became young again.

Perhaps it was the peculiar moral strength of the Archbishop, the leader of the Swedish church; perhaps it was the
man's astonishing fund of humor. Nathan Soderblom looked
ten years younger than his age. He had sparkling blue eyes,
yellow hair, a high forehead. Schweitzer was present when
Nathan Soderblom was due to officiate at the institution of
a priest in his benefice. The top of the Archbishop's crozier
had been left behind. It was thought that the ceremony
would have to be abandoned until someone had the idea of
inserting a flowering branch into the lower half of the crozier, and so, bearing the flowering branch, the Archbishop
proceeded with the ceremony, smiling jauntily.

To Schweitzer he was a well-spring of strength and a man
of resolute advice. It was Nathan Soderblom who asked him
to write a book on his African experiences and arranged for
a Swedish publisher. One day when they were walking in a
mild spring rain and sharing an umbrella, Schweitzer began
to talk of Africa and mentioned that he had accumulated
debts with the Paris Missionary Society. There were debts
to friends as well. He wanted to return to Africa, but how
could it be done? Nathan Soderblom smiled. He knew the
answer, and it was much simpler than Schweitzer had ever
imagined. "Give lectures and play the organ—that is all you
have to do," the Archbishop said. "The money will come
in, more than enough to take you back to Africa." When he
left Sweden, Schweitzer was making his first step back to
Lambaréné.

Yet sickness held him back—sickness and the *malaise*

which had been his constant companion since the first furious attack of dysentery in Bordeaux. To survive, he had to
drown himself in work, and the more he worked—he was
still tempted to work a sleepless twenty-four hours a day—
the more inroads there were in his physical resistance. Lectures and musical programs were arranged for him, but he
was determined to complete his first two volumes on the
philosophy of civilization. Exactly a year after his visit to
Sweden he resigned from his Strasbourg curacy and returned
to Günsbach, becoming a vicar to his father while he continued to work on the books.

There followed over a period of two years an astonishing
series of organ performances and lectures delivered before
applauding audiences all over Europe. He played the organ
in the Orfeo Catala at Barcelona at the first performance
ever given in Spain of Bach's *St. Matthew Passion*. He delivered lectures in Sweden, England, Switzerland, and
Czechoslovakia. He toured Denmark. London, Cambridge,
and Birmingham welcomed him. Before his first journey to
Africa, he had told himself he was prepared to sacrifice the
organ and the academic life to which he had given his heart,
and spend the rest of his life relying on the help of friends.
Now like Abraham he was spared the sacrifice; but like
Abraham he was to pay heavily for this blessing. He played
the organ and resumed the academic life to further the hospital at Lambaréné, but at a cost greater than he wanted or
could afford to pay. When he launched his lecture series, he
was still unwell, driving himself according to a stern and
stoic sense of duty, devoured by work and responsibilities.
He was like a juggler, balancing a hundred things at once.

He completed the two volumes on *The Philosophy of Civilization*, which appeared in German in the spring of 1923. He wrote his childhood memories and finished a small work called *Christianity and the Religions of the World*, an introduction to the vast work he had once contemplated. He practiced on the organ continually. All the time he was in correspondence with doctors and medical laboratories, theologians and psychoanalysts, teachers, pastors, publishers, musicians; always his mail was threatening to overwhelm him. He had the autocrat's temper: he must do it all himself, never delegating authority. By the end of 1923 he was nearly ready to embark. Almost to the last he hoped that Mme. Schweitzer would be able to accompany him, but she was still suffering from the illness which struck her at St. Rémy during the war. On February 14, 1924, he took the train to Günsbach and said goodbye to his father. Then, alone, he traveled to Bordeaux and sailed for Africa.

The ruined years were over: years of heartbreak, despair, sickness, a sense of mounting catastrophe. Now not fully recovered, but with more strength in him than he thought he possessed, all his boxes packed and his notes in order, he sailed out of the European winter into the summer of Africa.

~~~ 7 ~~~
The Best of Africa

THERE WERE PEOPLE IN Lambaréné who said he had not changed since the day he left them more than six years before. There were the same broad shoulders, the same heavy black mustaches, the same prominent chin and heavy nose and square chin. He walked with the lumbering stride of a peasant, and he had a habit of tilting his head back when he gave way to laughter. His eyes twinkled, and the gentle mouth under the thick mustache smiled easily. When they looked at him closely, they saw that the eyes had changed a little, showing evidence of the illnesses he had suffered, and there were small pouches under them. Sometimes, too, he walked a little stiffly. He was a man in his prime, nearly fifty, and as he came up the Ogowe river in the moonlight he had no worries in the world.

It had been a long, happy and carefree journey from Bordeaux on a Dutch steamer which called at twenty ports along the western coast of Africa—Dakar, Konakri, Freetown, Sassandra, Grand Lahou, Grand Bassam, Secondee, Accra, Lome, Cotonou, Fernando Po, Duala—the names sounded like a long Negro chant or like a litany. He was glad to be stopping at these ports. The truth was that he knew very little about Africa. He knew Lambaréné well, and had paid fleeting visits to Cape Lopez, but for a man who was regarded as an expert on all things African he was astonishingly ignorant about conditions outside the Gabon. So he stayed as long as possible in these ports, some of them obscure and rarely visited, taking notes, weighing conditions in one port against conditions in another. At Duala he left the ship and traveled into the interior, to Nyasoso in the British Cameroons, thinking he might one day take over the mission station abandoned by the Basle Mission and transform it into a hospital, but the venture came to nothing. To see the Resident, he traveled in the Cameroon Highlands 3,000 feet above sea-level and for the first time tasted the mountain air of Africa. Then, for as long as he lived in Africa, there were only the forest marshes of the Ogowe and the damp, low-lying river-banks and papyrus swamps, which breed mosquitoes and tsetse flies.

When he came in sight of Lambaréné, two months had passed since he left Europe, but it was still the rainy season in Equatorial Africa. The soft light of the full Easter moon fell on the dark water. It was very quiet as the stern-wheeler moved up river. At table the white timber merchants were still talking about timber prices and the difficulty of getting sufficient labor, but there were more ominous notes in their conversation later. They were talking about the leopard men —one of them had appeared two years before in Lambaréné itself, and nearly a hundred had been rounded up in the hinterland. Soon Schweitzer left the traders and stood at the rails, watching the river float by. Nothing had changed. The same broad river, the same decaying villages, the same forests, the same strange ancient landscape which seemed to have remained unaltered through countless ages.

He came to shore at midday on Easter Eve and took the long path up to the hospital like someone in a dream. For six years he had retained in his memory a vivid picture of the hospital as he had left it. The hospital had vanished. Instead of the wards which he had built with his own hands, there was grass and brushwood. The corrugated iron house which comprised the operating theatre, consulting room and dispensary remained, but its roof of palm-thatch had gone. The saplings he had planted had shot up. The paths were thick with weeds. Where there had been a clearing there was a young jungle. All, or nearly all, was lost in greenness.

With a sinking heart he realized he would have to start from the beginning. It was suggested that he should wait a day and rest, but he was in no mood for waiting. At three o'clock that same afternoon he began with the help of the young English college student, Noel Gillespie, who had accompanied him from France, to clear the jungle.

There were no carpenters at hand, so they did their own woodwork. There were no stitched-leaf tiles for the roofs, so they went off in a dugout canoe to a nearby village and flattered the natives into searching for discarded tiles—by the end of the afternoon they found sixty-four, but they needed hundreds. It was the rainy season, with the heavens opening every night, while the earth steamed in the sun by day. Without roof-tiles, he dared not leave his medicines in the hospital. Patients came streaming in. He had to leave them on the floor of the hospital. Two of them died of chills, because they were soaked in rain. Schweitzer began to demand to be paid in roof-tiles. It was a long fight. When an old chief came to the hospital to be treated for an injured hand, Schweitzer urged him to contribute tiles to the hospital. The old chief shrugged his shoulders and said he would deal with the matter when he returned home.

"No," said the doctor. "I can't wait. Tell the people in your village to send me three hundred tiles. It will help your hand to heal."

The old chief was furious. Three hundred tiles represented a fortune.

"I will give you a hundred," he said.

"Not enough," Schweitzer answered. "I want three hundred, but I will settle for two hundred. And not one less."

The injured hand was aching.

"I will give you two hundred on condition you treat my wound immediately."

Schweitzer treated his wound carefully, but the chief made no effort to have the tiles brought to the hospital. The days passed, and it became clear that the chief had no intention of sending for any tiles. Schweitzer battled with his conscience, and decided he would have to leave the chief's injured hand untended.

"You are not examining my hand," the chief complained.

"That's perfectly true. Of course, if you would have the tiles brought, it would help."

Anxious, the chief promised to have the tiles brought.

"You will have five hundred tiles brought?" Schweitzer suggested gently.

"You said two hundred, doctor?"

"That is true, but it was some time ago. I'm afraid I shall really need five hundred tiles altogether before I can be sure you hand will heal."

With such subterfuges was it necessary to work in those early days.

Schweitzer dreamed of a time when there were sufficient medical supplies, enough rice in the bins, enough wards for the patients. He knew even then that this time would never come. Once Goethe had written: "In our younger days we were sure we could build palaces for mankind. With experience we learn that the most we can do is to clean up their dunghills." Schweitzer was determined to clean up the dunghills.

As soon as the roof of the large ward was repaired, he set about building a new ward, where he could also store building materials, a washing boiler, bottles and tins—in Equatorial Africa bottles and tins assumed vast importance, for they preserved the objects they contained against rot and rain, damp and white ants, sun and mildew and all the exhalations of the earth. Quite early he developed an uncanny instinct for finding hidden bottles, and few things annoyed him more than a native's carelessness in not returning bottles. In nearly every letter written at this time he was crying out for storage bins, as though he hoped that in some mysterious way bins would fly out to him from Europe. For a while he was able to employ some friendly laborers loaned by a black timber merchant. There were five laborers and a foreman. They stayed only a few weeks, for their contract year expired and they went home. Then he was thrown back on volunteers from the hospital, finding them among the relatives of the patients and then cajoling them, promising them rewards, even threatening them a little. In the morning he would rouse them from behind their cooking fires, pleading with them to work, and in the evening he would solemnly collect their axes, hatchets and bush-knives and beg them to reveal what they had done with those they stole or carefully hid away.

So it went on, day after day, in the heat and the rain, and there was no rest. To make matters worse there was no dry season that year. Usually from May to September almost no rain falls during the day. That year the rainstorms came continually, so that the workers were up to their ankles in mud and the natives were unable to cut down and burn the vegetation for their banana plantations. Because the river was in flood, the natives could not go fishing. They were close to famine, with only a little fried fish left in the food stores. The Father Superior of the mission station would go out with a gun in the hope of returning with hippopotamus meat, but as likely as not he would be marooned on a sand-bank or caught in the rain in the swamps.

Up to this time Schweitzer had been in good health, but now the ulcers on his legs broke out again. The continual burning pain almost drove him insane. He hobbled about as well as he could, superintending the new buildings, knowing all the time that the moment he left the building sites the work would stop. He hated having to give up and stayed only for a short time in his own hospital: then he was back again, legs and feet bandaged, spending half the day on building and the other half with his patients. What alarmed

him was that there was little time to talk with the natives
and earn their friendship. "It would be so much better," he
wrote, "if we could sit round the fire with them and show
ourselves to them as men, not only as medicine-men and
custodians of law and order in the hospital." But there was
no help for it. All that year there was the continual fight
against the rains and the struggle to create new buildings and
the ever-present battle against sickness and pain.

And then the Bendjabis came, and it was worse—far
worse than Schweitzer had ever thought it would be.

The Bendjabis were small puny natives from the hinterland who had come to work in the timber-trade. They lived
in villages 250 miles away in the interior, in the hills and
the plains, far removed from the sweltering forests of the
Ogowe. They came in groups of fifty or a hundred at
the white man's bidding, poor homeless "proletarians of the
forest," men with no skill except the crude skill which came
with their puny strength. They were homesick, and hated
the dark forest, and they hated the river even more. They
had to work on floating logs: few of them could swim. They
knew none of the languages spoken on the shores of the
Ogowe. Suddenly removed from their ancestral villages,
where they had lived an effortless existence, they were a
prey to accidents and diseases. Now they streamed into the
hospital, and Schweitzer began to wonder whether he would
ever be able to catch up with their sicknesses and whether
he had enough food to feed them. Also, he could find no
interpreter, and he could rarely understand what they were
saying.

Much of their sickness they owed to the change of diet.

The European timber-merchants who employed them could give them only husked rice and dried fish. The husked rice gave them dysentery. They suffered from beri-beri and malaria: there were no mosquitoes in the high plateau country they came from. And Schweitzer could sympathise deeply with one of their most constant complaints—ulcers on the feet. They were undisciplined, difficult to control, perhaps rebellious, "beyond good and evil." They did not understand —how could they?—that hospital property was valuable: if they wanted to build a fire, they would simply tear down the beams of a hut instead of going to the edge of the forest and cutting down timber. They were "men who had become human animals, not merely savages, and living far from their homes and coming under so many injurious influences, they had sunk even below the level of savages."

Schweitzer was tormented by the problem the Bendjabis presented to him. The "injurious influences" were only too real; the sufferings of these poor skeleton-like creatures only too apparent. Yet he could not entirely blame the timber-merchants or the French authorities, who were careful to regulate the migration from the interior. They did not allow labor to be recruited according to the desires of the merchants, but insisted on the observance of an intricate set of laws, rules and regulations, to the despair of the merchants, who concluded that the administrators of the territory took no interest in trade. But in a very real sense the coming of the Bendjabis represented a form of compulsory labor. Schweitzer was in two minds about compulsory labor. He could not approve of it, and he could not disapprove of it. It seemed to him that there were times when compulsory

labor was permissible. Once he stated his position in a formula: "On the whole I find myself unable to disapprove of
compulsory labor: it is not wrong in principle. But I regard
it as impossible to carry out in practice." He was saying that
the ingrown sense of freedom of the African native prevented any real compulsion from being brought about. As
for "small scale compulsion" he could hardly disapprove,
since he employed it himself when superintending his building operations in the hospital.

When he came first to Africa in the years before the war,
he had given much serious thought to the problem. He asked
himself what would happen if some natives from the deep
interior were enlisted in compulsory labor service. Who
would provide food on the journey? Who would look after
them if they fell ill? Who would guarantee that the white
men could not call upon them just when the whole village
was setting about planting or going on its annual fishing ex-
pedition? Who would prevent the white men from keeping
them much longer than they had originally agreed? Now,
as he saw the Bendjabis in his hospital and realized that his
fears had been well-founded, he suffered an excruciating
agony of the spirit. It was terrible to watch the workings of
their untutored minds. He would tell them they must buy
mosquito nets and blankets, but instead they spent their
money on tobacco and trifles. They had their own wonderful
argument against buying useful things; they knew perfectly
well that Schweitzer would be forced to buy them for them.
So they stole and squandered and Dr. Victor Nessman, the
son of an Alsatian pastor, who had come out to assist
Schweitzer, complained: "How wonderful Africa would be

without these savages!" Schweitzer explained patiently and
at length that the Bendjabis, far more than the natives of
the Ogowe, represented the true heart of Africa. It was to
save the lives of the Bendjabis that he had come to Africa.

The rains and the Bendjabis corroded his temper. It was
the year when everything seemed to go wrong and when
there were never enough drugs for the patients, and not
enough food, and the river was always in flood, and too
many Bendjabis were dying. At the end of the year Dr. Nessman was suffering from boils and Schweitzer was tending
his ulcers, and saying over and over again: "The hospital is
not what it used to be." He was hopping about in wooden
shoes, because the ulcers prevented him from wearing
leather ones.

In the spring of 1925 there came a turn for the better.
A new doctor was on his way, bringing a nurse with him,
and at the end of January there arrived from friends in
Sweden a beautiful 28-foot motorboat called *Tak sa mycket*,
which means "Many thanks." With her narrow hull and
shallow draught, she was admirably equipped to navigate
the Ogowe river. Schweitzer was proud of her and never
ceased singing her praises, and he particularly liked the
tarpaulin awning which protected his head from the sun—
he had a deep and well-founded phobia against sunstroke.
He was particularly pleased because she was inexpensive to
run. By March two new buildings were up, a new doctor
had arrived, there were operations in the surgery three mornings a week and once more the hospital was fulfilling its
proper function. Schweitzer was looking forward to a long
and happy dry season when the storm broke.

At first it was a very small storm—nothing more than an increase in the cases of dysentery. By the end of June cases of dysentery began to increase alarmingly, and by the end of July there was an epidemic. At that time there were no known remedies for bacillary dysentery. Schweitzer, who had been hoping to spend more time on his study of St. Paul, found himself working twenty-four hours a day in an attempt to head off the epidemic. He had himself suffered from dysentery, and he knew how quickly resistance crumbled before it. He knew too that dysentery could be controlled only by stern measures. The patient must be kept clean, and he must never infect anyone else by touch or allow anyone to touch his personal possessions. Patients suffering from dysentery must be isolated from the rest. It was impossible to build isolation wards—there was neither money nor time, and there was no available labor. And as much as he tried, it was impossible to keep the patients from infecting one another. A Bendjabi suffering from ulcers would wander off to see a friend from his native village who suffered from dysentery. "So you want to kill yourself?" the doctor roared at him. The Bendjabi answered with quiet heroism and terrifying stupidity: "It is better to be with my brother and die than not to be with him." Against the desperate loyalties of the Bendjabis for one another Schweitzer labored in vain. They died like flies.

Schweitzer waged war against dysentery with bitterness and despair. He was fighting for something much greater than the survival of the hospital. He was fighting for the survival of all the riparian communities of the Ogowe. The epidemic was spreading like a flash flood. He was continu-

ally traveling up and down the Ogowe river to villages where
the epidemic had established itself, trying to cure the villagers with emetin, which at least had the virtue of curing
amoebic dysentery. And when he returned to the hospital,
it was only to learn that patients about to be released from
the hospital because they had been cured of their wounds
and illnesses had caught dysentery and died. One evening he
found a woman filling a bottle from the river at a place
where the water was most polluted. All the patients had
been ordered to get water from the fresh-water spring. But
no: the spring was some distance away, and she had thought
it easier to get water from the river.

As he tells stories of these days, his bitterness boils over.
However much he tried, he could not convince the Bendjabis to take elementary precautions. "It is useless to ask the
patients to be careful," he complained bitterly. "They simply
mock us! They take advantage of our overwork to show us
the worst side of their natures." So the complaints continue,
and the bafflement increases. Impossible to explain to them
the causes of the disease. Impossible to make them understand that the larva flourishes on the damp earth or in water
and burrows through the body until it becomes a worm eating away at the intestines. One day when he had heard for
the hundredth time of a patient drinking polluted water, he
sank back in his chair in his consulting room and groaned:
"What a blockhead I was to come out here and doctor savages like these!" Joseph answered quietly: "Yes, doctor,
here on earth you are a great blockhead, but not in heaven!"
Schweitzer commented: "He likes to give utterance to sen-
tentious remarks like this. I wish he would support us better

in our efforts to stop the spread of the disease." It is an odd comment, and it can only have been written in a mood of profound nervous irritation by a man at the end of his strength. As usual Joseph had said the sensible word.

It was the year when the heavens reeled. He had no sooner got the epidemic under control when famine marched across the land. The cause of the famine was the rain which fell in the dry season the previous year, preventing the natives from planting. Rice was imported, but the husked rice did not provide a good diet and contributed to the epidemic of dysentery; and in the interior few natives succeeded in obtaining rice, which had to be carried through hundreds of miles of forest on the backs of porters. In Lambaréné the famine was mild. A hundred miles away it was severe. Frightened and listless, weakened by undernourishment, the natives simply sat in their huts and waited for death. It was unthinkable madness. Schweitzer's bitterness knew no bounds. Forgetting that the natives were too weak to move, he asked sharply why they didn't arm themselves with spears and bush-knives and go hunting after wild pig. Hunting wild pig is not dangerous. The wild pig in the African forests are far less wild than those in Europe. Necessity is the mother of invention. That may be true of Europe, but it is not true of Africa. "No, in this country," Schweitzer wrote, "necessity paralyzes people into sheer idiocy!"

Soon the anger passed, for he could not have lived with himself on such a height of anger for long.

One morning he took the motorboat and went out alone upstream. There were so many pressing problems, and he wanted to think them out. When he asked himself why he had failed to stop the epidemic at the beginning, he always came back to the same answer—the hospital was too small to cope with the numbers of natives clamoring to come in. If the hospital could be enlarged, if there were more doctors, if there were more drugs and medicines—

He decided the time had come to build a larger hospital. Two miles upstream he came to the point where the Ogowe river divides into two broad arms. On the spit of land between the arms lay two abandoned villages on gently rising ground. Around these villages the forest had been cleared. Why not rebuild the hospital on these hills? Where he was it was impossible to expand; swamps, marshes and forests hemmed them in on all sides. He went to the District Commissioner and asked for a grant of this little spit of land amounting to nearly two hundred acres. He was a little surprised when it was given to him at once. That same evening he called the doctors and nurses together and informed them of his plan. He promised a new hospital large enough to cope with any epidemic that might arise: there would be isolation wards for dysentery patients, cells for the mental patients, more space, greater safety. They would have sufficient land for an orchard, and for growing cereals. He knew they would welcome the news, but he had not expected them to burst out cheering. The patients heard the shouts and wondered whether the doctors and nurses had suddenly gone out of their minds.

It was autumn now, with the rainy season coming on, the sky clear one moment, the next moment black with thunderclouds. With the District Commissioner's approval, it was decided to go to work at once. First, the ground plan was marked out, then some level ground was cleared so that maize could be planted—the threat of famine still hung over them. To cut down the forest, all the relatives of the patients were formed into gangs. Patients who could walk and those who had recovered were pressed into service. They worked willingly, because they knew they would be paid in extra food and the memory of the famine spurred them on. In addition to payments in food Schweitzer gave the good workers presents—spoons, cups, cooking pots, blankets, mosquito nets, sleeping mats made of raffia. They would have preferred alcohol and tobacco, but he had long ago set his face against such gifts.

Usually about fifteen workers set out every morning in canoes. Schweitzer would gaze at the tangled undergrowth and the enormous oil-palms, and wonder how fifteen workers would ever be able to clear the land.

The work went on steadily through the winter, with Schweitzer as foreman of laborers and chief building superintendent. When they worked well, he was deliriously happy; when they were lazy, he cajoled and threatened and made life miserable for everyone in sight. He was a hard but rewarding task-master, and he seemed to regard the undergrowth as a personal enemy, to be conquered by main force or by guile. They would come upon oil-palms thickly shrouded with matted vines. They would bore a tunnel through the vines and then lop them off near the roots. It was wonderful to see the choked oil-palms revive when the vines were cut away, but he complained over the wasted hours—sometimes it took a whole week to remove the hanging vines from the trees. The vines held the forest trees by the throat. In dead silence, they waged a strange and terrible war. Unless a tree grew above the height of the vines, it was inevitably strangled to death.

It pleased Schweitzer to set the work to music. In the first movement of the symphony the workmen, half-asleep, move at snail-tempo towards the bushes and trees they have been ordered to cut down. The second movement is *moderato*: axes and bush-knives moving in excessively moderate time. This movement ends with the midday break; most of the morning has been wasted. The third movement is *adagio*: "one hears from time to time the stroke of an ax." The fourth movement is *scherzo*: "merry words are exchanged, and a few workers begin to sing." The fifth and last movement takes place towards evening, when the wind begins to stir a little. "They hurl wild imprecations at the forest. Howling and yelling, they throw themselves at the forest. But—no bird must fly, no squirrel show itself, no question must be asked, no command given, for with the slightest distraction the spell will be broken."

Schweitzer's "Symphony of the Workers in the Lambaréné Forest" was not pleasant. There was too much gall and wormwood, too great a sense of frustration. It was a way to exorcise the demons of laziness and the corruptions of sloth. For him, hard physical labor was a drug, which calmed the spirit and gave strength to a flagging body. He had never expected that the task would be easy, and he was perhaps not surprised when it proved to be overwhelmingly difficult. There were armies of red ants in the thickets waiting to tumble on anyone who approached them. There were snakes everywhere. There were sudden thunderstorms, storms on the river, upset canoes, continual accidents, famine so close at hand that there were times when the workers had to be severely rationed. Even when the new hospital village had been built, a continual battle had to be fought against the forest and the river—the forest was trying to come back again, and every year the river would rise and threaten to submerge the plantation. The first year he lost some of his hard-won crops when the river rose. The hospital was built on piles and resembled a lake-dwellers' village. Schweitzer became something of an authority on pile-driving and on the proper way to char the piles, to make them last longer. It was backbreaking work, and he took more than his fair share of it, spending less and less time in the hospital. Ironically, he was turning his back on patients dying from the epidemic of dysentery or from the effects of the famine in order to spend time pile-driving. The forest obsessed him: he would cut deeper and deeper into it, to preserve the ground he had reclaimed, remembering in the swampy forest how Goethe had devised for Faust the task of winning back from the sea the land on which men could live and feed themselves. Speaking of this time of sweat and agony, he said later that he regarded Goethe as "my smiling comforter, the man who really understood." With a vengeance he was obeying Goethe's dictate "to dedicate oneself to worldly affairs and to leave none of one's powers unemployed."

The man who attempts to dominate the forest must be hard as steel and cold as ice. Schweitzer was neither hard nor cold, but he was determined to build the new hospital. So he struggled with himself, and at night, in the stifling heat, sleeping little, a prey to doubts and worries, he would

wonder whether the white traders were right. There were
white traders who told him he would be dead from
overwork if he continued his unequal battle with the
forest.

In January, 1927, the hospital was ready for occupation.
It was a gala day in Lambaréné, with motorboats churning
up the water between the old and the new hospitals. Flags
fluttered, there were streamers and bunting, everyone shouting and singing. Schweitzer spent the whole day supervising
the change. It was a brilliant day, with a cool wind blowing
—an auspicious sign, for there was rarely any wind on the
river except for a few brief minutes towards evening.
Schweitzer took the wheel of the motorboat and towed the
full canoes upstream, returning with empty canoes. In the
evening he made the final journey, to bring the mental patients to the new hospital. And when he made his last
rounds that night he heard from every fireside and from
under every mosquito net the cry: "We have good huts now,
doctor!" Now the patients no longer slept on bare earth
floors. "For the first time," he wrote, "my patients are
housed as human beings should be."

It was the hardest year he had ever known in Africa, or
was ever to know. Now the worst was over, and he was
beginning to think again about his book on the mysticism
of St. Paul, the inevitable successor to *The Quest of the
Historical Jesus.* He needed rest—a long rest somewhere
in Europe, and preferably in the hills of the Black Forest.
He needed to see his wife, who had remained in Strasbourg,
and he needed the company of white men, unless he was to
be sucked up into the clay of Africa. There had been too

many signs during that arduous year that he was breaking under the strain.

Still he had to go on. The new buildings had to be painted, to protect them from the weather. There were more logs to be charred and hammered into the earth, for piles. There were nearly forty huts raised on piles, each a yard from the ground, and most of them wooden-beamed, with timber walls and corrugated iron roofs. He could house 250 patients, and because the patients brought their relatives and friends with them the total complement in the hospital village was rarely less than six or seven hundred. It was a village meant to last, and he was justifiably proud of it.

He spent the next six months completing his plans. The epidemic of dysentery belonged to the past, and there was no more famine. About this time he learned that many unexplained cases which seemed to be dysentery were in fact a form of cholera endemic to the Ogowe region. Long ago, working on a hunch, he had treated these cases with argillacious earth dissolved in water, which is a specific treatment in cholera therapy. It pleased him to discover that his hunch had proved correct.

Other things pleased him. The hospital was thriving, no longer a nest of ramshackle buildings made of raffia and bamboo, decaying in the sun and the torrential rains. It was sturdy, well-built, well-organized—too well-organized perhaps, for the white traders and their wives instead of going to the government hospital at Cape Lopez began to flock to him. Now he had time on his hands: there was no longer that overriding compulsion to build huts and fight the forest and give sharp orders to unwilling workmen. He could spend longer hours over his lead-lined piano and enjoy the fantastic beauty of the African evenings and spend more time with his correspondence, which was always threatening to submerge him. So in the light of a kerosene lamp, in a small study strewn with books, with a dog or a cat on his knees, he would write half-way through the night. His handwriting had not changed with the years. There was no careless scrawl. The letters were small and round and firm, the last stroke as firm as the first. He almost never crossed out; he knew his own mind and where he was going. He was a man who finished whatever he started, deliberately, refusing to be hurried or harried, without impatience and without flourishes. He wrote with a thin margin on the left, but the words went across the page to the very edge of the paper: he wasted nothing, not even an inch of paper. And if the letter was long, the handwriting at the end was as firm as at the beginning. When the letter was finished, if there was more than one page, he jabbed the top left hand corner with a needle and threaded a little loop of black or white cotton through the sheets. In this hot humid land paper clips rust and he preferred these cotton threads which never rusted. He suffered from writer's cramp, which he inherited from his mother, but the letters show no signs of it.

He sailed for Europe in July. It was only when he was on the ship that he realized what a wrench it was to leave Lambaréné behind. As the ship nosed its way out of the bay in the bright sunshine—in Lambaréné two hundred and fifty miles away the sun lay hidden by the heavy clouds which make every July as dismal as London in the fog—

he gazed at the disappearing coast and it was like a sharp pain to think of the hospital he was temporarily abandoning. Gone were the teeming forests alive with apes and leopards, panthers and boa constrictors, gorillas and elephants. Gone was the huge river with its sandbanks and treacherous eddies, and all the hosts of ospreys and hawks and owls and cranes on its banks. Gone was N'Tschambi, the huge giant who had been brought to the hospital in chains because he went berserk and killed his wife with an ax, though now he was the most docile of patients and was allowed to wander unguarded into the forests with an ax slung over his shoulders. Gone was Joseph, his lean handsome assistant, who spoke wonderful French and derived his knowledge of anatomy from cooking, so that he was always saying: "This man's right leg of mutton hurts him" or "This woman has a pain in her upper left cutlet." It was Joseph who had warned and rebuked him when he was oppressed with nervousness and ill-temper, and it was Joseph who said: "The doctor is the slave of God, and I am the slave of the doctor." Gone were the morning mists and the blue haze over the forest and the reddish glow on the horizon on those evenings when the natives burned down the forest for their plantations. It was all gone, and he was not sure he would ever see it again, for he knew he was ill and might never be allowed to return again.

When he reached Strasbourg and consulted a doctor, his worst fears were realized. The doctor said he was suffering from nervous exhaustion. There must be no lectures, no concerts, only a prolonged rest. He bought a house at Konigsfeld in the Black Forest and began to write his book on St. Paul. The air of the Black Forest invigorated him, and within a week he had thrown the doctors orders overboard. He was ill, but he refused to countenance illness, just as he had refused to pay any attention to the warnings of those who said he would never succeed in building the new hospital. He defied illness. The demon of impatience (which does not show in his handwriting) took possession of him. Soon he was traveling over the whole length of Europe, giving concerts and lectures, never at rest, traveling everywhere in third-class carriages only because no fourth-class carriages were available. He gave himself four hours' sleep a day: he regarded these four hours as in the nature of a tribute to the gods of sleep, and he gave the tribute grudgingly.

He had three claims to men's attention: his knowledge of Africa, his playing of the organ, his books on Christ. So it would happen that in a single city he would be asked to play the organ and give lectures on Africa and Christianity. These were his major claims to men's attention, but there were many others.

In August, 1928, the city of Frankfurt-am-Main offered him the Goethe Prize "for services to humanity." The Prize had been given only once before, and then to the great German poet Stefan George. Schweitzer was asked to give a short address on Goethe. He described how throughout his life "Goethe was the comforter who constantly provided me with helping words." It was Goethe who had taught him not to be afraid of abandoning theoretical studies and immersing himself in practical affairs. Goethe had been by his side when he was a student, and in his medical studies, and in the teeming forests of Africa. Goethe was a modern of the moderns. "When the mail-coach was still crawling along the high road, and we should have thought the industrial age was announcing its arrival only by uncertain shadows cast in advance, it was for him already there. He was already concerned with the problem it set squarely before the world: the machine is taking the place of man." Schweitzer saw in Goethe a man who detested violence, an active moralist, imbued with ethical feeling. Consciously or unconsciously he was describing himself. It was the first of two addresses on Goethe delivered in Frankfurt and gives the impression of having been written hurriedly. Four years later there was to be another speech on Goethe, and this time Schweitzer spoke at greater length and with greater assurance, no longer overwhelmed by the strange image of Goethe as a transcendant moralist. The second Frankfurt speech is among the very best of Schweitzer's occasional writings.

With the prize money Schweitzer decided to build a house at Günsbach which would serve as a refuge for the nurses and doctors who had worked with him at Lambaréné when they returned to Europe, and as a retreat for himself. But he quickly changed his plan. Europe was at the beginning of the depression; there was poverty everywhere in Germany. And so he decided that he would give lectures and concerts in Germany until he had received a sum exactly equal to the prize money. The prize money he would return to the city of Frankfurt, to be spent on helping the unemployed; the money he received from the lectures and concerts would be spent on the house.

For a long time he had debated with himself about the house he had one day intended to build in Günsbach. His father was dead. A new pastor occupied the parsonage. He had a small apartment in the Rue des Greniers in Strasbourg and a tiny house in the Black Forest. He needed a house in Günsbach, but exactly where would he place it? He consulted friends, and went on mysterious journeys, examining the lay of the land, talking to farmers, and sometimes he spoke about "my house" as though it were already built. He considered himself a good architect—he had, after all, built two villages in Africa—and in the end he drew up his own designs, only consulting briefly with an architect from Colmar. The site he chose was close to the village square, within a stone's throw from the church, overlooking a rolling valley. Characteristically, he designed it so that the front door opened on the road leading to Münster, while the garden behind vanishes into the green and purple of the valley where he had wandered so often in his youth.

While the new house was being built, he worked at Konigsfeld on *The Mysticism of Paul the Apostle*, determined if possible to complete the work before leaving for Africa. The book had haunted him for more than twenty years and he was determined not to carry the manuscript back to Africa for the second time. But the work was continually being interrupted by visits to Holland, England, Czechoslovakia and France, and he did not complete it until he was on board ship, and he finished the very last pages on the river steamer taking him to Lambaréné.

He had been away for two and a half years, but the hospital had been well cared for in his absence. He was in good heart and good health, and this time his wife was with him. His days were as full as ever. He built a new house for mental patients, and began experimenting in concrete buildings —soon there was a concrete cistern and a concrete assembly hall for the hospital staff, which also served as a dining hall. People who had known him in the days when he was laying the foundations of the hospital, driving piles in the earth and managing his group of native laborers, found him remarkable carefree. The iron days were over. He was spending more and more time in the study of Indian and Chinese philosophy, and some of the gentleness of the Indian philosophers seemed to have grown into him. Once he wrote: "I can hardly remember a single day when I have delighted in being alive." But during this third visit to Lambaréné he was as happy as he could ever be.

Towards the end of 1931 the city of Frankfurt-am-Main asked him to deliver the commemorative address on the hundredth anniversary of Goethe's death. At first he was inclined to refuse. He had, he thought, already said all he ever wanted to say on the subject of Goethe. He was bound to the hospital, and in no great need of a rest. But in the end he decided to pay a short visit to Europe, and while still at Lambaréné he began to work on the speech.

March 22, 1932 was a gala day at Frankfurt, clear and sunny. There was no hint of the tragedy which would overtake Germany the following year, though there was poverty enough in the streets, and Schweitzer was not slow in noticing it. Yet there was an air of health in the city where Goethe had been born and where he died. Wreaths were piled before the statue in the Goetheplatz. Since early morning scholars, churchmen and civic dignitaries had been crowding into the Opera House, where the memorial tributes were to be delivered. The orchestra played the *Eroica,* and soon Schweitzer rose from his seat on the platform and began to speak on Goethe's message for our time. Speaking very solemnly he said:

A hundred years ago at nine in the morning, Goethe sat up in the armchair in which he had spent the night, believing he was recovering from his illness. He asked what day it was. Told it was March 22, he said: "So Spring has come, and my recovery will be all the easier."

He had forgotten one thing—he had forgotten that March 22 had always been for him a day weighted with destiny. He had forgotten the terrible March 22, 1825, when the Weimar Theatre, which he and Schiller had developed so brilliantly, burst into flames. He, the sun-worshipper, was overwhelmed with joy because the sun of spring was in the heavens.

His thoughts were already beginning to be confused, but he regained consciousness for a moment and begged them to open a shutter to let in more light. Before the spring sun had reached its zenith, he had entered the Kingdom of Eternal Light.

Today the city of Frankfurt is celebrating the hundredth anniversary of the death of her greatest son in the splendid sunshine of spring. We are celebrating at a time of the greatest anguish known to this city and to Goethe's fellow-countrymen. Unemployment, hunger and despair are the lot of so many people of the city and the Reich . . .

Schweitzer returned to the mood of those last words a little later, but it was necessary to sketch in Goethe's peculiar contribution to the city and to give a brief account of

Goethe's life, and to say some other things close to his heart, before continuing with the present time, the misery in the streets, and the face of the Führer pasted on the walls. So Schweitzer went on to tell the story of Goethe's life. It is a masterpiece of tact and affection. He is a friend talking about a friend. There is nothing weighty, nothing brilliant. He tells of Goethe worshipping God at sunrise beside an altar piled with fruit. He speaks of Goethe's abiding love for nature and the changing seasons, of his knowledge of guilt and redemption, of his ceaseless study of the natural sciences. He admits that Goethe was often in error. He could be curiously cold and daemonic, but for the most part he was warm and human and gently kind—Schweitzer was inclined to place Goethe on the side of the angels, and he quoted only the more religious passages from *Faust*. Yet the very affection with which Schweitzer embraced Goethe gave depth and understanding to the portrait. Towards the end of the speech Schweitzer raised his voice. Goethe had celebrated the integrity of the human soul, yet the present age was in danger of celebrating the death of the soul:

For what is happening in this terrible age is nothing less than a giant repetition of the Faust drama played upon the stage of the world. In thousands of flames the cottages of Philemon and Baucis are burning! In thousandfold acts of violence and thousandfold deeds of murder a spirit which has lost all human qualities wages its wanton game! With a thousand grimaces Mephistopheles leers at us! In a thousand ways men have allowed themselves to renounce their natural relation with reality to seek their gain in the magic formulas of economic and social systems which only make it all the more impossible for men to escape from economic and social misery.

And most terrible of all is the fact that these magic formulas, whatever the school of economic or social witchcraft they derive from, demand that the individual surrender his material and spiritual existence, and they allow the individual to live only when he belongs body and soul to a majority which absolutely controls him.

In the original German the cry is far more plaintive than it appears in English, and far more violent. *In tausend Flammen brennt die Hütte von Philemon und Baucis . . . In tausend Fratzen grinst uns Mephistopheles an . . .* It is Schweitzer speaking against fascism and communism, and at the same time he is speaking against the excesses of democracy, which he has never completely accepted, because he believes democracy powerless to affirm the worth of the individual human soul.

When the hour-long speech was over, there was a standing ovation, while Schweitzer remained on the platform with his head bent, saying nothing. He had called upon the ghost of Goethe to preserve Germany, and he seemed to know even then that Germany was doomed. He ended the speech with some lines from Goethe's *Hermann und Dorothea*:

> Aber es siege der Mut
> In dem gesunden Geschlecht!

> Now may courage bring victory
> To this healthy race!

But as he spoke them, the words sounded more like a valediction than an appeal to the heroic qualities of the Germans. All through the speech he had sounded the note of doom. "Remain human with your own souls," he cried. "If you surrender the ideal of human personality, then spiritual man is ruined, and with the end of spiritual man comes the end of civilization, yes indeed, the end of humanity!" Again and again he used the German word *"grausig"*— terrible—to describe the present age.

In the following year, when Hitler took over power in Germany, Schweitzer swore an oath that he would never enter the Third Reich. And whenever he spoke of Hitler, it was with scathing contempt. There, if anywhere, was to be found the mass-man whom Schweitzer despised. And when Hitler came on the scene, no one could deny the force of Schweitzer's prophecies of doom.

Usually his visits to Europe coincided with an intense desire to complete one of his books. This time Schweitzer was working on the third volume of his *Philosophy of Civilization*. As usual, he was able to do far less work on the book than he had hoped. There were constant, pressing invitations for lectures and organ recitals, and the universities of Europe were continually urging him to accept honorary doctorates—in one month in England he received four doctorates (two for divinity, one for music, one for laws) from three universities. He paid lengthy visits to England, Holland, Sweden and Switzerland, and seemed to have been endowed with the gift of perpetual motion. In university towns the broad-shouldered philosopher carrying his two linen laundry bags full of correspondence became a familiar figure. The University of St. Andrews offered him its rectorship; Glasgow gave him a civic banquet; the city of Stras-

bourg named a park after him. His hair was beginning to
turn, for the first time there were heavy wrinkles on his face,
but he still clambered up to organ lofts and sometimes he
would be seen cleaning the organ pipes with his own hands.
It was remembered that he gave an impression of extraordinary strength and gentleness, and was tyrannical only with
his translators, insisting that they keep the exact flavor of
his words when he spoke in public, hounding them until they
had exhausted every nuance of meaning and learned his
speech almost by heart; and since he often spoke German
with a pronounced Alsatian accent, and was not always
comprehensible to those who understood German well,
there were occasional quarrels. He demanded from his
translators the same unyielding obedience he demanded
from his gangs of laborers at Lambaréné.

He had come to Europe to deliver his speech at the
Goethe centenary and to enjoy a rest, but there was a little
rest. When he sailed for Africa in March, 1933, he was
exhausted. He was constantly falling asleep on deck, and
looked unwell. This time he paid only a brief visit to Africa,
and he was back again in Europe to take part in more lec-
ture-tours and to deliver the Gifford lectures at Edinburgh
and the Hibbert lectures at Oxford. At Edinburgh he met
Sir Wilfred Grenfell, the great missionary doctor who had
founded a hospital on the coast of Labrador. Schweitzer
tells the story of how they immediately began to cross-ex-
amine one another about the problems of their hospitals.
Grenfell complained about the loss of reindeer during their
migrations, while Schweitzer complained about losing goats
to snake-bite and theft. Then they burst out laughing: they

were not talking as medical doctors, but as farmers deeply concerned with the health of their livestock.

He left for Africa again in February 1935 and returned five months later, to complete the series of lectures he was offering in Edinburgh. Then there were more lectures, more concert tours—the old exhausting program was repeated, but the money kept coming in and with the money he was able to make further plans for increasing the scope of the hospital at Lambaréné. He worked on the proofs of a book called *Indian Thought and Its Development*—the Gifford lectures had been an attempt to trace the whole current of ancient thought in India, China and Persia, and this single volume was an elaboration of a few of his lectures. All the time he was searching out good organs and good doctors and nurses to send to Lambaréné. He was maintaining contact with doctors who specialized in tropical medicine, and spending more and more time with pharmaceutical advisers. By 1937 he was sure there would be a war—probably a world-war; and he needed a stockpile of medicines in Lambaréné. So he bought heavily out of his own earnings, and was continually sending to Strasbourg, the headquarters of all the supplies sent to Lambaréné, for more medicines, more bandages, more drugs. He was racing against time. He had fought for Lambaréné, and he was determined to fight for it to the end.

Three Books

A STRENUOUS SENSE OF RE-
sponsibility sent Schweitzer to Africa. He offered himself to
the service of the natives, but some part of him remained in
the world of ideas. He would try to tear himself away from
writing, and in Lambaréné he deliberately attempted to
keep his writing down to a minimum, but he could not prevent himself from thinking. So he continued writing, and
every night he entered into his notebook the thoughts that
had arisen during the day. He believed that thought, the
art of thinking out abstract problems, was a dying art, and
he was determined in an unthinking age to do his best to
rescue it from oblivion.

When the sun pelted the corrugated iron roofs of the
hospital and the heat came roaring out of the forest, he
was the doctor and the overseer; at night he became the
writer and musician. He saw no anomaly in this magical
change of countenance. This was how he was born, and how
he had to be; and he made no excuses for being a master
of so many trades. His first trade had been writing, and he
was faithful to it to the end. But whenever it came to draw-

177

ing up a balance-sheet of his life, he would regard his work in the hospital as the most profitable. At best a writer reaches only a comparatively small number of people. As a doctor in Lambaréné he became a legend and reached out towards millions of people who paid no attention to his books.

He said once that he could only be known by those who have known him in Africa. It was true, but it was not the whole truth. Of his eighty-three years only a little more than a quarter were spent in Africa. Seeing him in Africa, one saw a man continually improvising along a nerve, continually assailed by problems almost beyond solution, spending more and more time as a foreman of a gang of native laborers, planting vegetable gardens and orchards and pushing back the forest, more and more concerned with administrative problems, sometimes brutally impatient of the natives and at odds with himself, as though some kind of guerrilla warfare were being fought out within himself: a man whose essential simplicity was overlaid with furious complexities. He was a man of moods. He was at once the slave of Lambaréné and its patriarch. He loved Lambaréné with a desperate and overwhelming love, but he remained a stranger there. As the years went by, he complained increasingly about the difficulty of knowing the natives; they lived in realms beyond his reach; only when they were mortally ill could he penetrate at intervals into the strange world they inhabited, illuminated by the lightning-gleams of primitive cults and a fierce fetish-worship. He was no anthropoligist, and took little interest in their customs. Always he held himself a little in reserve.

Some who have known him well have suggested that there was good reason for his reserve. There were many qualities of the African native which he shared. Like them, he possessed a deep and abiding sympathy with nature. The peasant in him retained an element of primitive animism; a tree was more than a tree; it was a living thing which spoke to him and revealed its secrets, if he was patient enough, if he communed with it long enough. When he spoke of the sanctity of life—of all life—the philosopher was putting into philosophical terms the ancient animistic beliefs he had inherited from his ancestors. When he said that no blade of grass may be crushed, no icicle broken, no animal needlessly killed, it was because he believed that all life formed part of a whole and to injure any part of it is to injure the whole. When a native of the Ogowe cuts down a tree, he says a prayer to it and asks its pardon. Schweitzer would do the same. When he came to write about "reverence for life," he searched through all the philosophies and religions of the world to find substance for his beliefs, pleased when he found echoes of them in Christianity or in Chinese Buddhist texts or in the writings of the Jains. It is strange that he should gather so many quotations together, for there was no need for it. He had only to look out of his window to see among the natives attending his hospital the living embodiment of so many of his beliefs. He was closer to the natives than he knew. More than most men he had need to be reserved before them. Behind the theologian, the doctor and the musician was the smiling face of the peasant close to the earth, in a strange sympathy with the earth and all growing things, the winds of Creation flowing through him.

Something of this peasant quality is discernible in his writings. He has the peasant's formidable powers of concentration, and the peasant's plodding gait, and the peasant's defiance of intellectuals. He took nothing on trust. He would examine patiently everything that had been written on the subject he was studying, then go his own way. In his early writings there is nothing derivative. *The Quest of the Historical Jesus* passes in review all the available writings on the life of Jesus seen as a historical personage. At first sight nothing would seem less dramatic. One imagines a painstaking theological treatise buttressed by innumerable footnotes. In Schweitzer's hands it becomes an amazing adventure. He reviews the lives of Jesus written since the beginning of the nineteenth century, weighs them in the balance and finds them all wanting. With a superb gesture he then suggests his own convincing solution to the mystery, and having drawn a credible portrait of Jesus as He existed in His own time, he then dismisses the historical Jesus as irrelevant. He concludes that Jesus cannot be known historically. What is abiding and eternal in Him remains forever outside history, known to the spirit alone. "Who is Jesus? He has no name," said the German mystic Eckhart, and Schweitzer follows him. In a few concluding pages Schweitzer tears down the whole edifice so patiently and elaborately constructed by the theologians, who had sought to know Him who can never be known:

He comes to us as One unknown, without a name, as of old, by the lakeside, He came to those men who knew Him not. He speaks to us the same word: "Follow thou me!" and sets us the tasks which He has to fulfil for our time. He commands. And

to those who obey him, whether they be wise or simple, He will
reveal Himself in the toils, the conflicts, the sufferings which they
will pass through in His fellowship, and, as an ineffable mystery,
they shall learn in their own experience Who He is.[1]

In those words, the most poignant Schweitzer ever wrote,
and the most memorable, he came as near as he was ever to
come to the heart of the mystery.

In spite of its abrupt conclusion, *The Quest of the Historical Jesus* is a work which demands continuous attention.
It is a detective story. Schweitzer examines one by one the
writers of lives of Jesus for clues. He is no haste to come to
conclusions. It occurs to him that everyone who writes about
Jesus is valuable, even those who hate Jesus, and perhaps
those who hate Him are the most valuable of all. He shows
how the amateurs stepped in where the professionals feared
to tread, and were often more illuminating than the professionals. There was, for example, Karl Heinrich Venturini, the author of *A Natural History of the Great Prophet
of Nazareth*, published in four volumes embracing 2700
pages, in which all the miracles are explained rationalisti-
cally, and Jesus himself appears as a member of the Order
of the Essenes—a daring guess in the days before the Dead
Sea Scrolls showed a deeper connection between the Essenes
and early Christianity than anyone had suspected. Venturini's book attempts to relate Christ to His time. He tries
to put order into the disconnected fragments of the Gospels
and to explain the events as they happened. He was the
first of a long line of authors of lives of Christ, and Schweit-

[1] *The Quest of the Historical Jesus*, p. 403. New York: The Macmillan
Company, 1948.

zer gives him his due, praising him for his imaginative solution of problems. Venturini, though almost unknown and
forgotten, was the first to relate Christ to the circumstances
of Late Judaism and to establish a connection between His
teaching and contemporary Jewish ideas. Again and again,
as he discourses on the more famous Lives of Jesus, Schweitzer finds himself returning in admiration to Venturini and
to another immensely long work by Friedrich Wilhelm
Ghillany, who followed in Venturini's footsteps. Ghillany
believed that Jesus was a tool of the Essenes and that
Joseph of Arimathea was the mysterious Master of the Order, who contrived the condemnation of Jesus in the Sanhedrin. The Last Supper, according to Ghillany, was not
a Paschal meal but a love feast according to the custom of
the Essenes. Jesus goes to His own death in perfect awareness that He is the Son of Man promised by Daniel, compelling the secular power to put Him to death in order by
this act of atonement to win for the world the immediate
coming of the Kingdom. Schweitzer was particularly struck
by Ghillany's insistence upon placing the Life of Jesus "in
the last days," meaning that Jesus acted all through His
brief mission in expectation of the Kingdom. The orthodox
Lives had placed no particular emphasis on the Kingdom.
They attempted to explain miracles away, or to show the
Son of Man acting as a revolutionary leader, or to demonstrate His godlike powers; they had not seen Him living
in momentary expectation of the flames of the Last Judgement. Schweitzer regarded Ghillany's contribution as "an
historical achievement without parallel" and when the time
came for Schweitzer himself to suggest the pattern of Jesus's

life, he borrowed heavily from Ghillany's work, though
without borrowing Ghillany's affection for the Essenes.

For Renan's far more famous *Life of Jesus* Schweitzer
possessed no affection whatsoever. It was all landscape:
cornfields and whispering reeds and blue mountains. The
gentle Jesus, the beautiful Mary, the amiable carpenter
"might have been taken over in a body from the shop-win-
dow of an ecclesiastical art-emporium in the Place St. Sulpice." Christ robed in power and majesty becomes a charm-
ing prophet attended by devoted women, until He wearied
of them and a strange longing for martyrdom overcame
Him. Schweitzer's most biting comment comes with Renan's
words over the dead Christ. "Rest now amid thy glory,
noble pioneer," says Renan. "Thou conqueror of death,
take the sceptre of Thy Kingdom, into which so many centuries of Thy worshippers shall follow Thee, by the highway
Thou hast opened up." "It is all," says Schweitzer, "very
much as though he were standing in Père Lachaise Ceme-
tery and delivering a funeral oration on a defunct member
of the French Academy." Though he admired Renan's style
and half-regretted that the German writers of Lives of Jesus
had no sense of atmosphere or scenery, his final conclusion
on *La Vie de Jésus* is that "it was written by one to whom the
New Testament was always somewhat foreign, who had
not read it in his youth in the mother tongue and who was
not accustomed to breathe freely in its simple and pure
world, but must perfume it with sentiment to feel at home
in it."

Schweitzer had no sympathy for "the delicate Jesus" and
was determined to seek a solution in terms of "the last days."

About the middle of the nineteenth century the Jewish
apocryphal writings known as the "pseudepigraphia" were
being discovered by German theologians, and in the prophecies of Enoch they found an insistence upon the Kingdom
which puzzled them and turned their attention to the possibility of revising the accepted interpretation of the Resurrection and the Second Coming. Jewish Messianic ideas threw
light on the problem, and it was beginning to be possible
to reconcile Jewish apocalyptic material with the Gospels.
Schweitzer had found two clues in Venturini and Ghillany.
The third was in a remarkable treatise by Johannes Weiss
called *The Preaching of Jesus Concerning the Kingdom of
God*." According to Johannes Weiss it was necessary to
remove all modern ideas about the Kingdom, even in their
subtlest forms. The Kingdom must be regarded as wholly
future. It is present only as a cloud is present when it throws
its shadow on the earth. Jesus proclaims the coming of the
Kingdom—"Thy Kingdom come"—but it was never so
near as He thought. The evil, the impenitence and the
hatred in men's souls were barriers setting men apart from
the Kingdom. To destroy this barrier, to bring the Kingdom
nearer, He sacrificed Himself. So He died, not only for the
community of His followers, but for all people, for "the
many." After His death He will come again in all the splendor and glory which have been associated with the Messiah
since the time of Daniel, and the setting up of the Kingdom
will be preceded by the Day of Judgement. With the advent
of the Kingdom the world will be free of the world, all
human institutions will vanish and Christ will reign as the
Messiah. It was part of Weiss's interpretation that Jesus was

a man, a prophet, and the title "Son of Man" was no more than a tentative, temporary title to be employed on earth, while the dignity of the Messiahship belonged properly to Christ's rule in the Kingdom. Weiss's book was no more than 67 pages. But it was clear to Schweitzer that Weiss had reached the heart of the problem and his own interpretation borrows heavily from that remarkable pamphlet.

There were no lack of detractors who regarded Weiss's solution as invalid. The Jewish "pseudepigraphia" form an extraordinary collection of inspired utterances and rambling, disconnected prophecies. They were notably influenced by Persian thinking. By careful selection one could read into them any interpretation one wished. And so the battle rose between those who regarded the "pseudepigraphia" as Jewish mystical writings of no importance to the interpretation of Christianity and those who regarded them as of supreme importance. It was very much like the battle which rages today over the Dead Sea Scrolls.

Schweitzer held fast to the eschatological interpretation— the interpretation in terms of "the last days," the end of the world and the coming of the Kingdom. The problem was to attempt by scholarship and by an imaginative reconstruction of the time to discover the meaning to be attached to Christ's words. In the Gospels the words are bare, almost without associations. Reading the Gospels alone, it is impossible to understand the precise connotation of any of Jesus's sayings. The words must be clothed, they must be given accent and interpretation, they must be set to work. What is the Kingdom? Who is "the Son of Man," and who is "the Messiah"? A thousand questions arise, and it is part

of the virtue of *The Quest of the Historical Jesus* that
Schweitzer, instead of giving his own unsupported interpretations, tracks down the interpretations of nineteenth century theologians—those men of massive intellects—and by
sifting through the work and setting his own ideas against
theirs, he succeeds in refining an interpretation which is
among the most convincing ever offered.

As Schweitzer interprets the Life of Jesus, His mission
on earth occupied no more than a few weeks. It begins in
Galilee, where He makes known in the parables on the
cornfields that the coming harvest is the last, and is also
the token of the heavenly harvest. The end of the world is
at hand, and He knows Himself as "the Son of Man"—
the Transfiguration following shortly after the Baptism is the
God-given sign of His assumption of power. Yet in the
midst of His ministry He suddenly disappears, and His dis-
appearance remains inexplicable—perhaps He was afflicted
with doubts or felt that it was necessary to conceal His
powers. This last view, suggesting an intentional secrecy,
Schweitzer regards sympathetically. During this period He
becomes a "closed dark lantern, though not completely
closed—otherwise one could not see that it was there—
and there are a few bright beams escaping." These beams
are perceived by the disciples, yet they cannot quite imagine the fabulous light which lies concealed behind the closed
lantern. It is a time of intense strain and fierce expectation
of the Coming. "From the days of John the Baptist until
now, the Kingdom of Heaven is subjected to violence, and
the violent wrest it of themselves."

But it is the peculiar nature of Jesus that after dealing

in images of violence and suffering a violence of the spirit,
His earlier beliefs in the Kingdom of Heaven change. He
perceives quite suddenly that all is in the hands of God and
nothing that men do will affect the Coming of the Kingdom.
He becomes entirely passive, submitting Himself to the will
of God, though he retains the belief that the Coming of the
Kingdom will be at harvest time. So He sends out the disciples to make known to Israel, as speedily as possible, what
is about to happen. But it does not happen. The first grains
of barley are being reaped, but there is no Kingdom. It is
at this point that He decides He must offer himself up as a
sacrifice in order to hasten the Coming. So he goes up to
Jerusalem. He makes no Messianic entry in the sense that
the people acknowledged the triumphal entry of a Messiah.
"The entry into Jerusalem was Messianic for Jesus, but not
Messianic for the people." And once in Jerusalem or in the
neighborhood, there was no secret about His presence. If
the Sanhedrin wished to know where he was, there were
spies available. Judas did not betray Jesus; he betrayed the
secret of the Messiahship. "Jesus died because two of His
disciples broke His command of silence: Peter when he
made known the secret of the Messiahship to the Twelve at
Caesarea Philippi; Judas Iscariot by communicating it to
the High Priest." When Jesus admitted that He was the
Messiah, His doom was sealed. So He was crucified, as He
desired. "On the fourteenth day of Nisan—on the evening
of that day the Paschal lamb would be eaten—he cried
aloud and expired, choosing to remain conscious to the
last." He had died in order that the Kingdom of Heaven
might be brought nearer and to spare the Elect the suffering

of the Tribulation and to atone for believers who would otherwise have to be purified by suffering and dying. He had died in order that they might live, but the Kingdom of Heaven was still far away:

He seized the wheel of the world to set it moving on that last revolution which is to bring all ordinary history to a close. When he saw that it refused to turn, He threw himself upon it. Then it turned and crushed Him, and the wheel rolled onward, and the mangled body of the one immeasurably great man, who was strong enough to think of Himself as the spiritual ruler of mankind and to bend history to His purpose, is hanging upon it still. That is His victory and His reign.[2]

Schweitzer's portrait of Jesus is charged with romantic overtones. To the end it remains a poignantly personal portrait. The memorable passages in *The Quest of the Historical Jesus* are precisely those where the historical method is jettisoned and suddenly, quite effortlessly, in a mood of tragic elation, borrowing at a great distance from those who have gone before him, he reveals his own private concept in all its sustained glory. He sees a Jesus who failed to bring about the Coming of the Kingdom, but His death was no less heroic. "When he hurled the fire-brand which should kindle the fiery trials of the Last Time, the flame went out." So to the end Jesus remains for him a figure of titanic power, stark and tremendous against the sunset.

Soon after finishing *The Quest of the Historical Jesus*, Schweitzer turned his attention to a study of St. Paul, which he did not complete until 1929. Perhaps inevitably he saw

[2] *The Quest of the Historical Jesus.* By Albert Schweitzer. New York: The Macmillan Company. 1948.

St. Paul living in the light of the Last Days, a heroic figure
impatiently awaiting the Coming of the Kingdom. "From
his first letter to the last Paul's thought is always uniformly
dominated by the expectation of the immediate return of
Jesus, of the Judgement, and of the Messianic Glory." St.
Paul strains after the Kingdom. In a characteristic passage
Schweitzer speaks of St. Paul "taking the sacraments by
storm." And, curiously, St. Paul does not regard the Kingdom as a peaceful blessedness, but as a struggle with the
angelic powers. One after another these powers will be overcome by Christ and His people, until at last Death also will
be robbed of his power. The Kingdom, too, will come to an
end, whereupon Jesus surrenders his authority to God:

   In a tremendous paradox Paul puts in the place of reality, as
presented to the apprehension of the senses, the reality which is
valid for a thinker who understands clearly what moment in
world time this is. He knows that the immortal world is about to
rise by successive volcanic upheavals out of the ocean of the
temporal. In the resurrection of Jesus, "the first fruits of them
that have fallen asleep" (I Cor.xv.20), one island peak has already become visible. But this is only part of a larger island
which, still beneath the waves, is actually in process of rising,
and is only so far covered as to be just invisible. This larger
island is the corporeity of the Elect who are united with Christ.
In their transformation and anticipatory resurrection the further
portion of the immortal world will forthwith appear. Thereafter,
in temporarily separated upheavals, one portion of land after
another will rise round about this island. In the Messianic period
all nature will take on immortal being. And then, as the final
event of the renewing of the world at the end of the Messianic
Kingdom, will come the general resurrection of the dead. With
that the whole continent of the immortal world will have become

visible. Then comes the End, when all things are eternal in God, and God is all in all.[3]

This vision of the Last Days seen as a succession of volcanic upheavals is a staggering one, but Schweitzer is speaking about staggering things. For him the death and resurrection of Jesus are, as it were, no more than the curtain raisers to a cosmic drama of immeasurably vast proportions. The Kingdom of God becomes a place of unimaginable violence. There is no peace, no quietness anywhere. Yet meanwhile, according to St. Paul, men must live in Christ in the calm expectation of the Kingdom, facing sickness and death with imperturbability, for suffering and death bring men to fellowship with the death of Christ. Waiting, they must pray. Walking in the spirit, they are made new in Christ and the powers of death and resurrection already work in them.

At this point Schweitzer introduces into his study of St. Paul a consideration of Christian ethics seen in the light of the Kingdom of God. Jesus has died; the ethics of the former time are no longer applicable. Because the powers of death and resurrection are already at work, men are already entering into the spirit of Christ, daily dying in Christ. A new code is therefore demanded of them. In its simplest form the code demands that they should be Christlike. They must work to bring the Kingdom of God about. They must not withdraw from the world, but take their place in it. Theirs is the task to transform the world and bring it closer to the Kingdom of Heaven. The Judaic laws

[3] *The Mysticism of Paul the Apostle*. By Albert Schweitzer. New York: The Macmillan Company. 1955.

remain, but subtly altered; and above all other laws is the law that men should love one another. The law of Christ is compassion for all human beings, because all of them may in time come to live in Christ and enter the Kingdom.

Schweitzer's chapter on St. Paul's ethics may be regarded as a necessary introduction to his discussion of ethics in *The Philosophy of Civilization*, where he discusses "reverence for life" at great length. *The Philosophy of Civilization*, of which two volumes have already appeared—Schweitzer intends to complete the study with one more volume—attempts to trace the reasons for the decay of civilization and to suggest a cure. It is a work without much form, and with few passages of intense excitement. His studies of Jesus and St. Paul have heroic proportions and are illuminated with the lightning flashes of his intuitions. They become heroes, a thousand times larger than life, shining in the light of the heavenly sun. When Schweitzer discusses civilization, everything is in shadow. It is as though we were at the base of a dark mountain, at night, in the mist, trying to identify the shape of a strange city where only a few lights are shining. Schweitzer has no particular affection for the city. He lists and comments briefly on those who have written upon it before. The word "ethic" like a talisman appears on every other line. He collects a handful of the moral sayings of Epictetus and throws them on the page. It is an astonishingly pedantic work. But here and there, and most often when he is in a mood of acquiescence, he continues the argument of love which shines through the pages of his work on St. Paul:

There is no essence of being, but only infinite being in infinite manifestations. . . . Only an infinitely small part of infinite being comes within my range. The rest of it passes me by, like distant ships to which I make signals they do not understand. But by devoting myself to that which comes within my sphere of influence and needs me, I make spiritual inward devotions to infinite being a reality, and thereby give my own poor existence meaning and richness. The river has found its sea.[4]

At such moments he explains himself, seeing himself on the shores of the Kingdom which are also the shores of this world, and by implication explaining that "reverence for life" which brought him to Africa.

When Schweitzer discusses "reverence for life" in *The Philosophy of Civilization* it becomes almost a Kantian category. He can say, for example: "The reverence for life which has grown up in the will-to-live which has become reflective contains world- and life-affirmation and ethics side by side and interpenetrating one another." He is more human when he says:

You are happy, they say; therefore you are called upon to give much. Whatever more than others you have received in health, natural gifts, working capacity, success, a beautiful childhood, harmonious family circumstances, you must not accept as being a matter of course. You must pay a price for them. You must show more than average devotion of life to life.

Open your eyes and look for a human being, or some work devoted to human welfare, which needs from someone a little time or friendliness, a little sympathy, or sociability, or labor. There may be a solitary or embittered man, an invalid or an

[4] *Civilization and Ethics.* By Albert Schweitzer. London: Adam and Charles Black. 1949.

inefficient person to whom you can be something. Perhaps it is an old person or a child. Who can enumerate the many ways in which that costly piece of working capital, a human being, can be employed. Search, then, for some investment for your humanity, and do not be frightened away if you have to wait, or to be taken on trial. And be prepared for disappointments. But in any case, do not be without some secondary work in which you give yourself as a man to men. It is marked out for you, if you only truly will to have it.[5]

So quietly, leaving the insoluble problems of civilization aside, the wars in Heaven forgotten, he speaks like someone by the fireside.

[5] *Civilization and Ethics.* By Albert Schweitzer.

~~~ 9 ~~~
Torment and Plague

"FOR THE TRULY ETHICAL
man all life is sacred," Schweitzer had written long ago, and
in many volumes and at many different times he had demonstrated all the precautions which were needed to preserve
the little flame of life from extinction. Like another Moses
bearing the tablets of the law, he pronounced that all people had the right to live and develop at their highest poten-
tial, and even the humblest earthworm left high and dry on
the sunbaked earth after the rains must be lifted into the
damp soil where it can burrow. The moth must be preserved
from the candle, no flowers may be plucked and no leaf
may be torn. Now in Europe Hitler was stating categorically
that only one race and one nation had the right to live; all
others might be slaughtered with impunity.

It was the winter of 1938. Austria was already swallowed
up and Spain was crumbling. In the Sudetenland the Nazis
were beginning to undermine Czechoslovakia. Only a few
months remained before Hitler was to launch the greatest
war the world has ever seen.

In Lambaréné the great rains come in winter. Tornadoes

slash through the forests of the Ogowe. It is the time for
shoring up buildings and digging sluices. Roofs must be
strengthened, supplies must be carefully stored, patients
must be carefully watched, because the coming of the rains
brings on a kind of hysteria like the hysteria which affects
people in the Far East just before the coming of the mon-
soon. All day Schweitzer was at work, making his rounds at
the hospital, superintending the workmen. He wrote that for
a year and a half he had hardly been outside the hospital
grounds, and once again he was beginning to show the signs
of nervous fatigue. He was nearly sixty-five. He had not seen
his wife or daughter since the last journey to Europe. He was
beginning to debate with himself a problem he had hoped
he would never have to face. What if another war came?
In the first World War the hospital had collapsed. There
had been no funds, and he himself had been arrested and
sent off to an internment camp in France.

During a lecture tour in America in 1938 Mme. Schweitzer had raised a good sum of money for the hospital, but
there was no assurance that the flow of money would continue once war began. He had to think very seriously about
whether he would have to close down the hospital for a
second time. In this anguished state of mind he decided to
return to Günsbach and think out his problems afresh. It
had always happened that his mind worked best in his own
home, among the vineyards and the pine-trees of the Vosges
mountains. And Günsbach, he thought, would provide a
perfect sounding-board. There if anywhere, close to the
German frontier, he would be able to make a good guess
about the scope of the coming war.

On January 12, 1939, he left Lambaréné for Europe, intending to make only a brief visit of three or four months. If the hospital had to be closed, he would have to return to Africa. Worn out by the long preparations for the rains, he kept to his cabin, but he could not keep out the noise of the radio in the dining saloon, which was continually blaring the news of Hitler's latest threats. Hitler's name was on everyone's lips. At every port there were warships. He knew the German character and the German's exaltation in the face of war. Sitting there in his cabin he came to the conclusion that the war would almost certainly break out in June or July. In two great wars the Germans had set their armies marching across Alsace-Lorraine in summer. But when the ship steamed into Bordeaux harbor on February 1, he was not so sure. It might be a matter of a few weeks or a few days. He hurried to Strasbourg. In his apartment in the Rue des Greniers he summoned his closest friends and debated the coming war with them. Curiously, they laughed at his fears, but his mind was made up. He had read the newspapers. He could feel the war like a hot breath on his face. He was absolutely certain Hitler meant everything he said, and there was nothing in the world to prevent the wild beast from stretching out its claws. With his wife and daughter he made hurried trips to Günsbach and to Switzerland to buy supplies for the hospital, and on February 12 he sailed alone from Bordeaux on the same ship which had brought him from Africa. Three weeks later, looking gaunt and unrested, he climbed up the sandy shore of the Ogowe and made his way among the coffee trees to his hut. The nurses and patients were stunned to see him back so soon.

"Is it war?" he was asked, and he answered: "Yes, it is war."

His mind was made up. Though there were hardly enough funds to maintain the hospital, and very little hope that the hospital would survive if its source of funds dried up, he was determined to keep it going, even if it meant maintaining it in a restricted form. Sick at heart, he began to draw up a blueprint for the future. By every possible means, employing all the resources of the hospital, it was necessary to assemble large quantities of drugs. He sent out orders, marking them urgent. He examined his stocks and attempted to work out a plan by which they could be made to last for seven years—he had an odd feeling that the war would last seven years, and in this he proved to be nearly right. He worked on hunches. He bought up huge quantities of rice from the traders at the ports who thought there would be no war, or if there was a war the sea-lanes would be kept open, and were therefore prepared to sell him their second-best rice at bargain prices. The traders thought the usual supplies from French Indo-China would be coming in throughout the war, whatever happened. The second-best rice was always tainted with weevils, but that was a small matter. Schweitzer bought up enough rice to fill the small granaries at Lambaréné to bursting. Drugs came in on every boat. It was a period of intense preparation. During the spring and summer four of his best nurses and doctors left him, to return to Europe, but he still thought he could carry on. When the war came in September, he was prepared for it and the blueprint was immediately put into operation.

September is the last month of the dry season. That

month the hospital was completely reorganized. Because the rains were coming soon, and because it was necessary to see that patients who could not be kept in the hospital returned safely to their homes, he had to make harsh changes. Reluctantly, he had to send home patients, even those suffering from hernia and elephantiasis, who could not be cared for in the hospital. Those who were not seriously ill were taken down to the river-boats that stopped at Lambaréné or were given small gifts of food to keep them alive during the homeward journey through the jungle trails. Operations were cut down to a minimum. It was heartrending, but it had to be done, and he was glad when it was over. And just as reluctantly as he dismissed the patients, he had to receive inside the hospital compound some of the white women who lived in lonely jungle outposts and whose husbands had been mobilized for war.

Now the hospital was no more than a ghost of itself. Only a handful of native laborers and field workers remained. Only two trained doctors, Schweitzer and Ladislas Goldschmid, the authority on elephantiasis, remained. Through November and December came the great annual storms, when the palm-trees swung furiously from side to side, and the river rose, threatening to drown the whole hospital. From the radio came ominous news that Hitler was preparing to launch the blitzkrieg on France.

Once again Schweitzer was faced with the questions of the natives about the European war. This time he was no more successful than he had been in the past to explain why white men killed one another. He felt helpless before their questions. All he could say was that something terrible and

incomprehensible was happening, that war was a disease
which afflicted people and drove them into a state of madness, so that they altogether forgot the commands of Jesus.
And he feared that the war would do irremediable damage
to the authority of white men in Africa.

Occasionally there was good news. On January 11, 1940,
Dr. Anna Wildikann, who had already spent three years at
the hospital, arrived at Lambaréné after a resourceful escape from Latvia, and in the same month the Swiss nurse,
Gertrude Koch, arrived from France by air. Then in March
the *Brazza*, which had taken Schweitzer on so many voyages
back and forth from Europe, was torpedoed off Cape
Finisterre, and with her went the last consignment of drugs
and surgical equipment sent to the hospital from France.
She sank quickly; there were almost no survivors; and soon
it was known that many of those who were drowned were
people from Lambaréné returning to French Equatorial
Africa.

It was a big blow, and there were to be many more blows
during the long hot summer.

France fell, and the Governor of Gabon threw in his lot
with Vichy. In all of French Equatorial Africa only Gabon
held out against the Free French. By October the forces of
the Free French and the forces of Vichy were fighting at the
gates of Lambaréné. Mercifully, both commanders agreed
to spare the hospital, but stray bullets kept falling on the
hospital compound. Schweitzer ordered the staff and patients to place sheets of galvanized iron, used for roofing,
against the sides of the houses. Some patients hid behind
the galvanized iron sheets while others took refuge behind

the thick concrete walls of the water cistern. Little damage was done, and by the end of November De Gaulle's army was in command of all the territory of Gabon. With the Gabon in the hands of the Free French, all communication with France was cut off. It was a blessing in disguise, for now the sea-lanes were being opened for communication with America and England, and through England with Sweden, where in the past much help had been forthcoming.

Now, with the war won in Central Africa, the hospital could once more take its proper place in the community and there was no longer a pressing need for retrenchment. Then, too, there were a large number of white patients clamoring to be treated. A fantastic number of white patients, grown anaemic from their long sojourn in the tropics, had to be treated for calcium deficiency and gastric ulcers. There was so little lime in the water available at Lambaréné that kettles in which water was boiled never became furred, and because there was no pure water anywhere in the tropics, it had to be boiled, and the boiled water never contained lime. So the patients received calcium orally and by intravenous injection, and had to be watched closely. Gastric ulcers were commonplace, and when they ulcerated they had to be treated immediately. Usually the proper drugs were at hand. The trouble, according to Schweitzer, was caused by lack of cooking fats, for all the cooking was done in palm oil, which contains acids. There were malaria cases, and more cases of deep muscular abscesses, those terrible abscesses which break out inside the muscle itself and multiply and are so difficult to seek out. With penicillin most of these diseases could have been kept easily under control, but there was no penicillin at Lambaréné in those days. And Schweitzer himself was suffering from anaemia and trying to keep it under control with preparations of iron and liver extract.

The war had caused untold harm to Gabon. Its economy was ruined. Trade in lumber, cocoa, coffee and palm-oil came to a standstill. Having lost the Dutch East Indies to the Japanese, the Allies were in desperate need of rubber, and now the old rubber trees deep in the forests were being tapped again by gangs of native laborers sent off to work in primitive camps. It was nearly thirty years since the natives had worked these rubber trees. They had lost their skill, and hated the work, and were careless. So from time to time there came to Lambaréné patients from the far-off forests suffering from strangulated hernia or snake-bites or maulings from forest animals. Often their cases were hopeless, and they came to the hospital only to die.

The war however brought one distinct advantage to the Gabon. The allies were determined to push through the building of a great highway from Cape Town to Algiers by way of Leopoldville and Brazzaville. The road passes through Lambaréné. So much work had already been done on the road that when in the summer of 1941 Mme. Schweitzer escaped from France and made her way on a Portuguese vessel to Angola, she was able to make the journey from Angola to Lambaréné in record time. For this Schweitzer was grateful, but there were few things which happened during the war for which he felt any need for gratitude. Detesting the war, there came a time when he could hardly bear to have the war mentioned in his presence, and he banished radio sets from the hospital. For war news he relied on a hand-written bi-weekly bulletin issued by the authorities in Lambaréné.

By the end of 1941 the hospital contained nearly as many patients as it contained before the war. Drugs were already beginning to run out. There were big gaps in the shelves. But from 1941 on money began to arrive from America, England and Sweden, and though no new supplies of drugs and surgical instruments reached the hospital, there was at least the money to pay for them. Through Dr. Edward Hume of the Christian Medical Council and Professor Everett Skillings of Middlebury College orders were placed for large consignments from America. The weeks, the months passed. Schweitzer was at his wits' end, thinking they must be at the bottom of the sea. They reached him at last in the spring of 1942. There was more than he had dared to hope for— rubber gloves, household utensils, thermos flasks, huge boxes filled with the latest pharmaceutical instruments. There were drugs whose existence he had never suspected. And with these treasure-chests there came an invitation to spend some months of much-needed leisure in America.

Schweitzer shrugged off the invitation. True, he was tired out. There was hardly a moment of the day when his body and his brain were not being exercised to the full. After the collapse of the lumber trade, swarms of unemployed native workmen were wandering about Lambaréné with nothing to do. He decided to employ them in building hundreds of yards of strong stone walls to protect the shores of the hospital from sliding into the river. He would reorganise the orchards and cut down the brush and clean up the streets,

which were full of pot-holes as a result of the rains. He became a large-scale employer of native labor, and except
for the hours he spent in surgery in the morning and in
making his rounds, he devoted himself to forestry, road-
repair, dyke-building and the care of the orchard, which
flourished so well that he was able to produce a surplus.
Part of this surplus he gave as a gift to the people of Lambaréné, urging them to eat more fruit. "Fruit," he said, "is
the best medicine in the tropics." Now that there was a large
orchard at his command, he made all the patients eat fruit-
salads liberally, and in the dining-halls there were heaped
bowls of oranges, grapefruit, tangerines and pineapples.

If this love of fruit were an obsession, it was one he
admitted to gladly. Over the years thousands of young fruit
trees had been raised in the nursery; now there was the
opportunity to experiment in planting and seeding on a
massive scale. He threw himself into the task, supervising
the cultivators as he supervised the road-menders, the ditch-
diggers, the dyke-builders. Somehow—he never quite knew
how—he succeeded in being everywhere at once. "I have to
be the patriarch," he said. "It is the only way, and I am
sure the Africans have need of a patriarch." But if he was a
patriarch, he was one of the most energetic ones who have
ever appeared in Africa. One moment he was giving orders
to the men breaking stones for the dyke, the next he was
pointing out the best way to fill pot-holes, then he would be
seeing that the wood was being properly fired in the kitchen
and the laundry. He was a good mechanic, and could repair
the pumps if they failed, and mend tools (the natives were
always throwing tools away as soon as they broke) and set

the refrigerators going. But above all, it was the orchard which delighted him.

He had theories about the growth of fruit-trees, and defied anyone to disagree with him. For example, he insisted that when an orange tree is planted there must be a hole one metre square and 80 centimetres deep with 20 centimetres of humus on top. If asked why the hole must be exactly 80 centimetres deep, he would answer: "Because it is so, and if you knew anything about husbandry, you wouldn't ask silly questions." He acquired a large library of books on agronomy and an immense collection of seed catalogues. There were some who said he was more in his element as a farmer than in any of the other occupations he had mastered.

Meanwhile the war went on, the work constantly increased, and the strain was beginning to tell on him. By 1944 he began to realize how really tired he was. It was not only the heat. He was overworking and the mental strain and responsibility were almost more than he could bear. "Henceforth," he wrote, "we had to draw on our last reserves of energy in order to meet the demands of the hospital. Not to fall ill—to keep fit for work—this was our constant, daily care. It was clear to all of us that none of us must collapse, for there could be no replacements for a long time." About this time—for exercise, and also so that he could keep control of the far-flung operations of the hospital —he would be seen *running* from one end of the hospital grounds to the other.

All this time the familiar plagues tormented him. There were the long winter days of thundering rain and the continual war against white ants. There were days when white

ants appeared as though by a miracle in the most inaccessi-
ble places. They were found on the shelves of the dispensary,
in the rice bins, in the lumber yard. They were nibbling
away at bandages and papers and beams. As soon as they
were discovered, there was a hue and cry, and all the resources of the hospital were thrown against them. The important thing was to discover where they came from, what
was their particular means of ingress: then this would be
sealed off. He had tried everything he could think of to
exterminate them, but even DDT proved of little help. He
could speak kindly of leopards, refusing to kill them, merely
saying he had a good reputation among leopards for being
a fencer-in-of-chicken-runs. But against white ants he raged
unceasingly. They were the only insects he ever called
"wicked."

He was constantly being reminded that he was living in the
heart of the jungle. Some miles up the Ogowe there was a
tribe which supplied the hospital with bananas. Twice a week
dugout canoes, heaped high with the bright green bananas,
came to the landing-stage. Sometimes the dugout canoes
failed to arrive, and some time later it was learned that a
herd of elephants had been trampling down the plantation.
Sometimes a native would come staggering into the hospital,
mauled and scalped by a gorilla. And one evening, while
Schweitzer was working at his table, he looked up to see a
full-grown panther staring at him through the window. There
were lighter moments. Once when he was supervising the
setting up of boundary posts, he thought he heard the voices
of women and children. He was far from where women and
children might be expected to be, and called out to the

natives, asking them what women and children were doing in this remote corner. The natives only laughed, and pointed to the crowd of chattering chimpanzees in the forest, all of them excited by the presence of the laborers and by Schweitzer's full-throated voice. At such moments he could forget the war: forget the concentration camps where so many of his friends had died: forget London and the bombings and the deaths of so many young men who should have been spared for better things. But there were not many such moments.

Weariness set in. There were inexplicable depressions wnich had to be fought off with all available stratagems. "Sometimes our feet drag as though made of lead," he wrote to a friend. And in the report which he wrote covering the war years at Lambaréné, he wrote:

We confided to each other that we all had to make an effort to pull ourselves out of our constant depression in order to be able to carry on the daily work. We all constantly felt it incomprehensible that while other people were condemned to suffer or to be active in ways that must cause suffering and death, our own job was one of giving compassionate aid. The realization of this privilege gave us daily fresh strength for our work and made it precious to us.[1]

For Schweitzer and those around him the worst period of the war was the summer of 1944. Supplies were coming in, but they were almost at the limit of their strength, and to make things worse there were heavy rainfalls in the dry season. The river rose, and the natives were prevented from

[1] *The Hospital at Lambaréné during the War Years: The Albert Schweitzer Fellowship,* January 1947.

burning over the forest they had felled, so that it was impossible for them to lay out new plantations. By good fortune an intelligent forest officer had insisted upon the planting of rice as far back as 1942, when fear of a food shortage was already being felt. But the economy of Gabon, nearly ruined by the war, was not improved by those torrential rains which made 1944 a rain-drenched nightmare.

On January 14, 1945, Schweitzer celebrated his seventieth birthday. The British Broadcasting Corporation announced a special broadcast in his honor. For once Schweitzer permitted himself to listen to a radio. He heard the Oxford theologian Dr. Nathaniel Micklem discussing the theories which were first put forward in *The Quest of the Historical Jesus* and then there came one of Schweitzer's own organ recordings. Schweitzer was pleased. He nodded his head in time with the rhythm of the organ, and when the broadcast was over he rose abruptly and returned to his rounds. He remembered afterwards that it was a stifling hot day, one of the hottest days he had ever known, and that he spent the afternoon worrying over several heart cases and performing an operation on a patient suffering from strangulated hernia who had been brought in that morning.

Four months later, he was sitting at his writing table after lunch finishing some urgent letters when a white patient, who had brought a radio to the hospital, shouted that according to a report from Leopoldville in the Belgian Congo an armistice had been concluded in Europe on land and sea. It was about 1:30, and the letters had to be taken on board a river steamer by two o'clock. He wrote his letters hurriedly, despatched them to the steamer and went off to see some urgent cases: the usual two o'clock appointments had been made and he was determined not to break them. When he had dealt with the heart cases he ordered the big gong to be sounded, summoning all the patients who could walk to meet him outside his hut. Then he told them the war was over, said a prayer, and dragged himself off in spite of a great fatigue to the plantation to see how the work was going on. For Lambaréné it had been a day like every other day.

It was another hot day, and there was little relief in the evening when he returned to his books. His wife was with him. He took down from the shelf the little volume of the works of the Chinese philosopher Lao-Tzu and began reading aloud:

Weapons are evil and should be shunned by the noble spirit. Only as a last resort does the noble man take up his weapons, for he loves peace above all things.

He takes no pleasure in victory. He who rejoices in victory rejoices in the slaughter of his fellowmen.

In the time of victory, the victor should comport himself as though attending a funeral. A multitude are killed, and tears should flow for them. That is why the victor should comport himself as though attending a funeral.

~~~ 10 ~~~

The Last Years

THE HOT SUNLIGHT BEAT
down on the thatched roofs of Lambaréné. The air was
motionless. There was no wind, and if the palm trees
stirred, it was only because a faint pulsating rhythm moved
through their branches. For ten days, for twenty days a
man could look at a palm-tree and not detect a single movement of the leaves except an almost invisible ripple. At
midnight the thermometer showed that the heat had not
changed since the middle of the afternoon. Day after day
in the long dry summer season the earth seems to be standing still.

In Lambaréné nothing had changed. The hospital had
survived two wars, but it was still living on credit. There
were not enough doctors or nurses. The same difficulties
which faced him when he first came out to Africa continued
to face him day after day. He bought rice wherever he could
lay his hand on it, he kept guard over his dwindling supplies
of drugs and he pulled strings. Prices began to shoot up. He
made calculations, and soon came to the conclusion that the
cost of carrying on the hospital would increase fourfold

209

within a year or two; however many strings he pulled he could not alter the ineluctable laws of economics, trade recessions and spiralling prices. Already the mission schools in Lambaréné were closing down, and now once again he had to face the possibility that the hospital, which had survived so many threats to its existence, would be forced to close.

Help came, at first in dribbles, then in small floods. From America especially there came money and drugs, while from Alsace and Switzerland, where he was most widely known and where his followers were most faithful, came nurses and doctors. In those early months following the end of the war, the hospital survived by a series of miracles, and there is astonishingly little difference between the reports he wrote at this time and the reports he wrote thirty years earlier. No complaints: only a sense of brooding weariness and bafflement: the Africans are in need, and how can I bring them what they need when my resources are so small? He wanted to build a leprosarium, but there were no funds for it. Leprosy indeed had become one of his special studies. English experiments with diphtheria-toxoid, French experiments with a drug obtained from a plant found in Madagascar (*Hydrocotylus asiatica*) and American experiments with a drug called promin, which was related to the sulphonamides, were promising. He hoped—it was one of those fierce hopes which swept through him from time to time—to gather all the lepers in the neighborhood within a leprosarium on the hospital grounds and stamp out the disease once and for all. But all this seemed to belong to the remote and improbable future, and meanwhile he was growing old.

Years before, returning to Europe, he had thought of himself as one who was completely forgotten, "swept under the furniture to be out of sight." So from time to time in his letters, together with the hints of weariness and strain, there came hints of foreboding. Somehow, in some way not clear to him, the hospital must be kept alive.

In 1947, looking more patriarchal than ever, he was still at his post. The fierce black mustache had turned white, the face was thinner, but the powerful massive body retained its vigor. He still walked with great loping strides, and still slept only four or five hours at night. Old age had not affected his playing of the piano: the massive wrists and powerful fingers were as flexible as ever. But a change was coming over him. There were notable signs of mellowing. He could be—he often was—categorical and Olympian, but now it was observed that he laughed at himself a little more often. In the old days a period of relentless strain might last for months: everyone was aware of the huge depression which hovered over him like a thundercloud. But having survived two wars, he had learned the trick of thumbing his nose at depressions. Above all, his orchard gave him intense pleasure. As he wandered through the lanes of trees, digging his heavy boots deep in the earth, admiring the blossoms and the fruit, he was the peasant again, descendant of the *vignerons* who had cultivated the Münster valley. Of all his accomplishments, planting fruit-trees was the one which gave him the greatest pleasure.

About this time his fame in America went through a re- birth. Long forgotten, his slightest statements made head- lines. And he began to suffer some of the disadvantages of fame. Elderly American ladies began to descend upon him, demanding to receive from his lips the secret of greatness. He put them to work in the hospital laundry and suffered them gladly, because he needed all the help he could get. Reporters found the hospital flourishing, and returned with lists of statistics and excellent photographs of the world's most photogenic hospital. There were 40 buildings, beds for 350 patients, three doctors, six nurses, 10 native assistants, and a small insane asylum 150 yards from the main hospital. It gave every impression of thriving. It was. But only because miracles were occurring. In that same year Schweitzer was writing despondently: "It will be very difficult to keep the hospital going. When we think of the widespread and still incalculable impoverishment in all directions, we have good reason to doubt whether it can last much longer."

By the summer of 1948 Schweitzer was thinking hopefully of making a journey to Günsbach. His wife was ill. He had spent nearly ten years in Africa without a vacation. He needed a rest, mountain air, leisure to complete the third volume of *The Philosophy of Civilization,* which was to be known as *The World-View of Reverence for Life.* He wanted too to see the four grandchildren who had been born during his long absence. If possible, he hoped to raise enough money to build the leprosarium which had become his fondest desire. So, in October, he sailed for Europe, giving himself a year's leave of absence. He hoped to spend most of it in the Black Mountains. He had not counted that his return would be something of a triumphal march.

He reached Günsbach towards the end of October, and

almost at once he was deluged with invitations. Most of
them he could toss into the large musette bag which served
as a repository for his correspondence, but there were some
invitations which he could not in propriety refuse. Günsbach
wanted to fête him. So did the town of Kaysersberg, where
he was born. So did Colmar, where he first set eyes on
Bartholdi's heroic Negro. Strasbourg begged him to accept
the keys of the city and Strasbourg University urged him to
attend solemn ceremonies in his honor. He accepted these
invitations and refused a hundred others. A little to his sur-
prise he had become "the great son of Alsace." There were
parades and speeches. He was pleased when they were over,
and he could get back to work on his book. Every evening
visitors to Günsbach or Konigsfeld in the Black Forest could
see his shaggy head bent over the lamp as he worked.

The bi-centenary of Goethe's birth took place in 1949.
To commemorate Goethe in America, a group of enthusiasts led by Dr. Robert Hutchins decided to hold a festival
in the former silver-boom town of Aspen, high up in the
Colorado Rockies. Invitations were sent out to the leading
intellectuals of the world. They were asked to make speeches
and to accept a fee. Schweitzer, whose name was being
increasingly coupled with the name of Goethe, was inevitably invited. He was at Günsbach, working quietly at his
book, when the first invitation came. He waited. He was
in no hurry to accept. He wanted to write his book and rest,
and he had no particular desire to climb up the Colorado
Rockies. A second invitation arrived, then a third. Each of
the letters offered a fee of $5,000. Finally, there came a tele-
gram, offering to make the hospital at Lambaréné a gift of

$6,100 (2,000,000 francs) if he came to Colorado and made two speeches on Goethe. For five days Schweitzer wrestled with his conscience, unable to eat or sleep. Then he accepted. On June 28 he arrived in New York on the *Nieuw Amsterdam.* It was his first, and only, visit to America.

When he arrived he was treated as the celebrity of the day. Reporters, photographers and newsreel men crowded round him. He was hailed as "the man of peace" and compared favorably in sermons with Lincoln. He was asked to comment on the American scene, but he laughed off the questions. A rugged, heavily built man, red-faced, with a great mane of snow-white hair, he was photographed on the ship's deck against the New York skyline. For once the New York skyline was not disgraced. He looked what he was, an Alsatian peasant of phenomenal strength of will and unerring intelligence; and the reporters, accustomed to meeting show-girls, showed an open-mouthed respect verging on awe. He was asked whether he regretted the sacrifice of his life to the natives of Africa. He answered: "There was no sacrifice. I am one of the greatly privileged."

On the journey to Colorado, it pleased him sometimes to play the wise old peasant. He traveled with Dr. Emory Ross, the treasurer of the Albert Schweitzer Fellowship, an elderly bright-eyed man who had long been one of his close friends. Dr. Ross was surprised to find that Schweitzer kept his money in a little string-bag. "Ah," said Schweitzer, "I will tell you the secret of the bag. It was given to me by my mother. I found out why she gave it to me the first time I was eating at a restaurant with my schoolmates. It takes

time to unwind the strings round the bag, and long before
I succeeded in untying the strings, someone else had paid
the bill." Then he roared with laughter.

He was in good spirits during the journey. He reached
Aspen on time, though delayed by a rockslide. The festival
was scheduled to last from June 27 to July 16, but his own
speeches were to be delivered on July 6 and July 8, one in
French closing the first part of the festival, the other in
German opening the second part. During the journey he
had worked hard on the French translation of the speech.
He sweated blood on the train. He was determined that the
speech should be delivered faultlessly, and he was perfectly
aware of the gravity of the occasion. Never before in Colorado, and hardly ever before elsewhere, had there been
gathered in one place so many glittering talents. The musicians Artur Rubinstein and Gregor Piatigorsky were there.
Dr. Ortega y Gasset, the philosopher and novelist, was making his final public appearance before his death. Dr. Ernst-
Robert Curtius had flown in from Germany. Thornton
Wilder represented the American stage. All had come to
celebrate the name and fame of Goethe, and in their presence Schweitzer was oddly humble.

When it was time for Schweitzer to deliver his speech, he
was still nervous, still humble. He described Goethe as "one
who points the way to victory over the demoniac spirit."
Goethe was a clean wind blowing through the murk of
Europe, the one Olympian who stood above the European
tragedy. He pictured Goethe as the enemy of the Faustian
myth; and if there were few who could bring themselves to
agree with him, everyone was delighted to hear the thick

rolling Alsatian accents. When the speech was over, and while he was standing back to receive the applause of the audience, Schweitzer turned to the friend who had accompanied him on the journey, beamed and said proudly: "Weren't you proud of my Parisian French?"

Everyone was proud of him. He was fêted and garlanded. Someone asked him why he did not stay longer in America and look at the American countryside. His eyebrows rose, and he shrugged the question off, saying he would begin sightseeing when he was seventy-five. In Africa he had sighed for high mountain air, but Aspen, 7,900 feet up, was too much for him and he complained of the difficulty of breathing in high altitudes. He asked politely for "the assistance of the local witch doctors." Then he was off to Chicago to receive another honorary doctorate in law to add to his collection. He was back again at Günsbach before the end of July, delighted with his reception in America but glad to be free of reporters. Before sailing, he explained that every penny of the fee had been spent on supplies of promin diasone, the American drug which had exceeded all the expectations of its discoverers in the fight against leprosy.

Now at last he felt free to organize a determined campaign against leprosy at Lambaréné. When he returned to Africa in October, the blueprints of the leprosarium were drawn up. There was still not enough money to pay for it, but at least the drugs were in the dispensary.

It was the eighth journey to Africa. He was close to his seventy-fifth birthday, but he looked younger than he had looked for some years. There were minor annoyances. Gil-

bert Cesron's film *Il est Minuit, Docteur Schweitzer,* with
Pierre Fresnay acting the leading role, was nearing comple-
tion, and Schweitzer had grave doubts about any films based
on his life. He did not enjoy seeing films, and until quite
recently detested being in front of a camera. Once long ago
a film-maker making a short documentary of the hospital at
Lambaréné had cut into a shot of the Ogowe river a shot of
another river in French Equatorial Africa. Schweitzer's
eagle eye detected the substitution at once. It was explained
that there was almost no difference between the two rivers.
No one outside of central Africa would have the least awareness that two rivers had been involved. Schweitzer regarded
the substitution as "grossly unethical," and set his face
against film-makers in general, only to capitulate a few years
ago when Miss Erica Anderson, a young Hungarian photographer, penetrated the fastness of Lambaréné and showed
him that the movie camera in sympathetic hands was ideally
constructed to show the most delicate glimpses of the human
soul at work. For years he had been thundering that the
camera showed nothing except the outward aspect of things
—it could not penetrate into the depths. Miss Anderson
showed him how it could be done. She wrote the scenario
for a film about the hospital at Lambaréné. Schweitzer
glared at it, tore it to shreds, completely revised it, and
then threw himself into the task of making movies. The
Gilbert Cesron film however still irks him. It is a sentimental
film based on a stage play, and in his view gives only a
superficial portrait of his work in the hospital. It has not been
shown in America, and it is unlikely that it will be.

Meanwhile he was determined to take the first steps in

building the leprosarium. He borrowed and scrimped, and the first buildings were already going up when he returned to Bordeaux from Africa on June 8, 1951.

If he had wanted to, he could have measured the growth and diminutions of his fame by examining the crowds who came to greet him when he stepped ashore in France. There had been a time when only policemen had greeted him, to lead him off to an internment camp. This time the crowds were greater than ever. He had half-guessed he would receive another ovation, and tried to conceal the date of his arrival, but the journalists already knew the date. The crowds screamed and roared. Reporters boarded a pilot launch and met him while the ship was still steaming into harbor. Carrying his own luggage, he fought his way through the crowds to the third-class compartment which would take him to Alsace. Another rest. Another attempt to get the notes of *The World-View of Reverence for Life* into order. Another round of festivities, and another breathing space. As he grew older, he hoped to spend longer intervals in the Black Mountains and the forests of the Vosges, but he could never foresee a time when he would remove himself completely from Africa.

There were the usual fêtes in his honor; he had long ago given up hope of escaping them altogether. In Frankfurt-am-Main, President Theodor Heuss of the West German Republic presented him with the Peace Prize of the German Association of Publishers. The prize was ten thousand marks. It was good news: he was a little nearer the completed leprosarium. Honors were coming thick and fast. The French Academy offered him the seat previously occupied by Marshal Henri-Philippe Pétain. Schweitzer was keenly aware of the irony by which the arch-traitor of France and the former glorious defender of Verdun was replaced by a doctor from an obscure corner of Africa, a former inmate of a French internment camp. He accepted the high honor gratefully, only begging to be excused from making the traditional visits to the Immortals and he asked to be forgiven for his absence on the day of election. The election was set for December 3, 1951. On that day he was far from France. He was in fact at Konakri, the capital of Guinea, where his ship had put into port, and he was playing the church organ for charity. Then he sailed on to Lambaréné: the leprosarium: the long fight to keep the hospital going: the winter rains: old age coming on.

One day in 1952, when he was working on a ladder, struggling to put up a corrugated iron roof on one of the buildings in the leprosarium, there arrived an emissary from Stockholm. The emissary was spotlessly dressed, Schweitzer was in his usual rough clothes. At first Schweitzer was a little nonplussed. There was some talk about the weather, and Schweitzer interrupted to give orders to the native helpers.

The emissary was saying: "I have come from Stockholm, sir, on a matter of——"

"All right, hold that end of the roof!"

The emissary made himself useful. A little while later he mentioned that he had been sent by the Nobel Prize Committee to inquire whether Schweitzer would accept the Peace Prize and whether he would be able to come to Stockholm to deliver the required acceptance speech. That year the

Nobel Peace Prize amounted to 171,570 kroner or about $33,000.

"I'll come," Schweitzer said. "Not now, but when I can. And give them my thanks. I'll use the money for the leprosarium."

Then he went back to work on the roof.

From that time the work on the leprosarium went on by leaps and bounds.

Previously the lepers had been housed in bamboo huts with sloping raffia roofs. Raffia grows brittle in the sun and rain. Good bamboo is hard to get. At best these huts have to be rebuilt every three years. Visitors to the leper village were sometimes headed off: the huts looked tattered, and the lepers rarely took much care to keep them in good condition. Schweitzer had long ago hoped to provide them with permanent dwellings. The flimsy huts would be torn down. Instead there would be houses with concrete foundations, hardwood beams to resist termites and corrugated iron roofs projecting far out, so that the lepers could stay in the shade when out of doors, and behind each house, some fifteen feet away, there would be a cooking hut. He wanted to build houses the lepers would be proud of, and at the same time he wanted by good design to show the natives how to build a model village. Previously the leper village was on the slope of a hill some twenty minutes' walk away from the main hospital. The winter rains came roaring down the hill every year: the huts were flooded: and in winter the natives were kept busy repairing the raffia walls, while the rain came down. Now Schweitzer proposed to level off the top the hill and use the earth to build up the sides. It was the kind of operation that cried out for three or four bulldozers. Instead, even with the money coming in from the Nobel Prize, he would have to use native labor.

Work on the new site began in May 1953. A friendly timber merchant made a loan of light rails and rail trucks. The rails were laid on the slope, and the natives were delighted. You filled up a truck with earth and let it race down the side, after leaping on. It was a new game, and they played it brilliantly, rarely getting injured, though there were enough minor accidents to make Schweitzer fear for the future. In the end he decided he would have to assume the role of foremen of rail trucks. In addition he was his own contractor and his own overseer. Once again he was in command of an operation for which he had no particular training but immense skill. And as usual, he was continually complaining about their laziness and carelessness. The stone-cutters sat in the shade of the mango trees, telling stories. There were long intervals when the only sound was the droning voice of the story-teller. Or they would answer their names at roll-call, only to vanish—they would disappear into their huts or go fishing, or slip away into the darkness of the forest. He knew all their ruses; he knew when they were really working and when they were simulating work. If there were four or five natives working together, it was always best to keep an eye on them. He wrote:

Before any job is started, you have to make sure they bring the right tools with them. You have to remember what is needed on the site, see that the men get it from the stores and bring it with them. They think nothing of going off with a shovel, or dropping a pick to lighten the load. Much time is lost putting all this to rights, time which cannot be made up, and sometimes the work never gets properly going for the day. When the bell sounds for quitting time you have to make sure that all the tools are returned. On the site you have to see that everything is in place, and at the toolshed that everything is handed back. And it is not enough to see that you have the right number of bush knives; you have to make sure that they are the right ones and not old and useless ones instead of the good ones that were handed out, and the same is true of axes, saws, picks and shovels. If rain starts suddenly while the men are at work, you have to stop them from just running off and leaving their tools lying around where they could be lost or mislaid.[1]

It was an old complaint, going back to his earliest days in Africa, and though he raged against the incompetence of the natives when they worked under him, he could be remarkably patient. Not all were lackadaisical: there was the old carpenter Monenzalie, who had helped to build the original hospital thirty years before. It was Monenzalie who put the corrugated iron roofs into place, with his team of four helpers—an old grizzled grey-haired man who retained his skill and took a passionate delight in his work. Then there was Obianghe, a former leper, who bossed a gang of native workmen and took it hard if he was called upon to do anything but weaving raffia, but on weaving raffia he was the world's expert. There were not many native workmen Schweitzer trusted; and he inveighs against their criminal laziness more often than he praises their dependability.

For Schweitzer their insufferable laziness was their greatest fault, their quiet dignity their greatest virtue. Unhappily,

[1] *Eight Year Report on Lambaréné Hospital:* 1946–1954. *Albert Schweitzer Fellowship,* 1955.

the one was involved in the other, and as they stood about
the building sites, their dignity was an offense against the
dignity of work. To subdue the land—that, for Schweitzer,
had been the task of civilization from the beginning. The
mark of the civilized man was not that he built airplanes and
railways, but that he built sturdy houses and cultivated ripe
fields. The natives understood the making of machines remarkably well: they simply put it down to the ineradicable
cleverness of the European. But when they came to Europe,
it was the sight of endless ranges of plowed fields which
stirred them, as it stirred Schweitzer, to the depths. In his
war against the laziness of the African, Schweitzer sometimes seems to be continuing his war against himself. Never
rest! Never give up! Through work a man comes to his
fullness! And whenever he appeared among the native workmen, the familiar gruff voice could be heard saying: *"Main-
tenant, au travail!"*

The work was now going apace, and with the building of
the leprosarium the hospital at Lambaréné increased its
scope and grew to almost double its former size. More and
more workmen were being employed. The hospital, once a
small village, was becoming a fair-sized town. In this town,
as in the village, Schweitzer was mayor, chief medical officer,
chief surveyor, superintendent of all buildings and all rice-
bins. He was foreman in charge of levelling operations and
exercised the functions of *garde-champêtre*. He looked after
the dispensary. He led the interminable attacks launched
against white ants. He gave the appearance of being everywhere at all times: the natives still regarded him as a man
possessed of superhuman powers. He worked on his books,

and played on the piano, and still had time to greet the lowliest guest at the hospital. And nearly all the correspondence that came to the hospital was written to him, and nearly all the letters that went out of the hospital were written by him. No wonder he was tired out! In the summer of 1954, excusing himself for an unusually long silence to friends in America, he wrote: "The war years have been hard, but those that followed were harder still. With the best will in the world, I could only do a part of what had to be done."

By the end of the summer of 1954 the greater part of the preliminary work on the leprosarium was over. Nearly half of the buildings had been built; the concrete was laid; the roofs were on the rafters. For a long while the Nobel Prize Committee had been urging him to come to Oslo to receive the medal which goes with the prize. Now at last he felt free to make the journey. He arrived in Oslo on November 2, 1954. There were torchlight processions by students. It was observed that he was unusually grave, and though he smiled often there was a gravity in his smile which gave him more than ever the appearance of a patriarch who had emerged from another age. Norway was at the beginning of its long winter. Schweitzer had come out of the summer of Africa to receive the prize.

In the speech he delivered two days later in the presence of King Gustav Adolf, he made his last impassioned plea for a peace which would preserve the dignity of man. He followed his accustomed practice of stating the history of the problem and briefly passed in review all the efforts which had been made in Europe since the sixteenth century to form a league of peaceful states. The figures of Erasmus and

Kant were summoned out of the ghostly past into the formidable present. On Kant especially he dwelt at length, and with a kind of brooding affection, for had not Kant said that a reign of law would come about when Nature, "the great artist," worked upon mankind—very gradually and over a very long period of time—until the march of history and the horror of war persuaded men to agree to an international covenant guaranteeing perpetual peace. But Kant failed, and those who came after him failed, and to Schweitzer this was all the more astonishing because the eighteenth century, the time of enlightenment, had put an end to witchcraft, torture chambers and superstitions. Oddly, Schweitzer makes no reference to the witchcraft, torture chambers and superstitions of the present day. What is needed, he says, is another great outburst of the human spirit comparable to the great outburst in the eighteenth century. We have only one resource. We must seek out the human spirit: we must create a new personal civilization in which reverence for life and reverence for the spirit go hand in hand. He said:

The human spirit is not dead; it lives on in solitude. Because it has been compelled to survive without the knowledge of the world which would correspond with its ethical character, it has somehow contrived to do so. It understands that it must base itself on nothing but the essential character of the human being. Now that it is stripped of all other knowledge, it is all the stronger for being naked. The human spirit knows that compassion, in which all ethics must be rooted, only attains its full flowering when it embraces all living creatures and is not only concerned with mankind. The old ethic did not possess this depth, this strength of conviction; and now there has come into being a new ethic—that of reverence for life—and the validity of this new ethic is more and more widely acknowledged.

He may have been whistling in the dark: there was little evidence that the new ethic had come into being or taken any of the world's fortresses by storm. And later on in the speech Schweitzer indicated that we are still waiting for this ethic to appear. We are, he says, living through an interim period, and the first sign of this manifestation of the spirit will be the resolution by all nations to repair the wrongs they have committed. When the hundreds of thousands of interned prisoners have returned to their own homes; when those who have been unjustly condemned are acquitted and when all the other uncounted injustices have been set to right, we may hope to see the spirit manifesting itself. Schweitzer demanded above all that there should be an elementary confidence among nations, and he despaired of this confidence as long as injustices remained. He believed the human spirit capable of creating a new attitude of mind, an infinitely more ethical attitude than it possessed previously. Believing this, he could only repeat his fundamental belief that the time had come for this spirit to manifest itself, for if it does not, humanity will perish.

There was little new in the Nobel Prize speech. Much of what he said was already contained in his book *The Philosophy of Civilization*. What was new was passionate invocation of the eighteenth century, the age of Kant and Goethe, before vindictive nationalism rose to torment Europe and before men assumed control of vast mechanical processes of destruction. Kant had been so superbly convinced of the need for a League of Nations, and so certain it would come about, that he repeatedly insisted it would be a mistake to introduce the ethical argument. Men would come to this simply because it was in their practical interests. Schweitzer answered that this was the supreme flaw in Kant's argument. For him, the ethical law alone possessed validity, the practical interests of men being too often misguided. Above all there is the law: thou shalt not kill. But how shall that law be invoked when man, possessed of superhuman reasoning powers, is so lacking in any awareness of the moral law:

Man has become a superman, and suffers from a fatal imperfection of the spirit. He is not raised to a superhuman level of understanding which corresponds to the possession of superhuman strength. He lacks the capacity to put his gigantic power to work for rational and useful ends; instead he puts his power to work for destructive and murderous ends. So it happens that the advance of science, instead of being advantageous to him, has proved fatal to him. . . .

Only now does the full horror of our position become clear to us. We can no longer evade the problem of the future of mankind. The essential fact should now strike home to us (and it should have struck home long ago) that inhumanity is the constant companion of the superman, and progresses as he progresses. We have tolerated the mass killings of men in time of war—about 20,000,000 in the second World War. We have tolerated the annihilation by atomic bombing of whole cities and their populations; and we tolerate the use of incendiary bombs and the transformation of men into living torches. We have learned of these things by radio or from the newspapers, and we have judged them according to whether they signify achievements accomplished by the society we belong to, or whether they were done by our enemies. When we admit that all these things are direct results of acts of inhumanity, we qualify the admission that "war is war," and there is nothing we can do about it. So, by offering no resistance and by resigning ourselves, we become guilty of a crime against humanity.

The important thing is that all of us should acknowledge that we are guilty of inhumanity. The horror of that avowal must arouse us from our torpor, and compel us to hope and work for an age where there will be no war. These hopes, these determinations, can have only one object: the attainment, through the growth of the spirit, of a state of superior reason in which we shall no longer put to deathly uses the vast powers which now lie at our disposal.

As he spoke, Schweitzer was well aware that he was saying things that had been said many times before. In the eighth century B.C. the prophet Amos had startled the Jews with similar prophecies of doom. The great Chinese philosophers, Lao-Tzu, Mo-Tzu, Confucius and Mencius had threatened destruction upon the kingdoms which refused to follow "the Tao." Tolstoy had repeated these warnings; and like Schweitzer Tolstoy had brooded deeply on the works of the Chinese. Schweitzer was only the last of a long line of thinkers who had seen the cracks and flaws in civilization, and saw no hope unless there was a violent regeneration of the spirit. But he claimed one originality for himself:

The only originality I claim for myself is that for me this truth is accompanied by the certainty, born of thought, that the spirit is capable in our epoch of creating a new attitude of mind: an ethical attitude. This certainty persuades me to affirm the truth anew in the hope that my testimony may prevent men from believing that this is no more than a well-intentioned formula. More than one truth has long remained ineffective simply because no one imagined it could ever become realised.

This was his only claim to originality: that he had re-
stated the problem in terms of the present, according to the
truth that was in him. Here were no attempts at brilliance.
Solemnly, earnestly, he demanded that men should turn to
spiritual things, that they should safeguard the integrity of
the individual and strive for justice. Politicians, whose lives
were living proof that they had no desire to turn to spiritual
things, nor to safeguard human integrity, nor to achieve
justice, had very often said the same words. Few in our
modern age had said them with Schweitzer's authority.

At the very end of the Nobel speech, Schweitzer warned
the rulers of the world against playing with the lives of
their subjects, and characteristically he invoked St. Paul:

May those who have in their hands the fate of nations take
anxious care to avoid whatever may worsen our situation and
make it more dangerous. And may they take to heart the words
of the Apostle Paul: "If it be possible, as much as lieth in you,
live peaceably with all men." His words are valid not only for
individuals but for whole nations as well.

It has been worth while to discuss the brief Nobel Prize
speech—in its printed form it occupies only ten or twelve
standard-size pages—because Schweitzer was quite deliberately attempting to resume in a few pages a whole lifetime
of thinking on subjects close to his heart. He was no Colum-
bus; he had not discovered any new land. He possessed no
spells with which to allay the hungry heart of man. But he
gave profound meaning to words which had lost their meaning, which had become worn out with use. When he spoke
of "reverence for life," he spoke with the authority of a

230 THE THREE WORLDS OF ALBERT SCHWEITZER

master, for he had himself given the phrase its modern relevance. And when he spoke of "the fatal imperfections of the spirit," he spoke with the authority of a man who had studied those imperfections at length in his two published works bearing on the decay and rebirth of civilization. In the course of a brief speech, there are six separate occasions in which he employs phrases like: "Civilization is doomed unless . . ." or "We shall all perish if . . ." He was deadly serious, and meant every word. "The ground," he told a Norwegian journalist, "is shaking under our feet. It is like an earthquake. And what are we doing to prevent ourselves from being engulfed in it?" But in the great hall where the speech was delivered, he received a standing ovation and was cheered to the rafters. He received the medal and was complimented by the King. The fate of the modern John the Baptist is to be applauded at court, and no Salome dares to demand his head on a silver salver. His ears ringing with applause, he stumbles out of Herod's palace and communes with his God.

The torchlight processions and the festivities were over. He stayed for a few more weeks in Europe, but he detested the cold winters and looked forward to spending his birthday in Lambaréné. On a sunny afternoon in December 1954, with five tons of equipment for the new leper village at the hospital, he sailed away from Bordeaux.

He spent his eightieth birthday at his post in Lambaréné. Congratulations poured in from all over the world, but he was in no mood to enjoy them. When he was asked to take part in world-wide radio broadcasts, he said he was exhausted, he had a heavy schedule at the hospital and there were still more buildings to be erected. The strong, craggy face was looking stronger and craggier. Increasingly, as the years passed, he was finding himself at home in Africa, far from the European tragedy.

In Africa he traveled little. For years on end he was content to live at Lambaréné. In all the world there were only two places he called his home: the obscure village in Alsace and the hospital on the Ogowe river. And he was determined to die there. Like the natives who died in his hospital, his body would be covered with a cloth shroud and he would be let down into a shallow grave, the green palms of victory lying on him. He called it "the green coffin," and he was content with it. But sometimes—and it usually happened towards the end of summer—he would find a need to see Günsbach at harvest-time. So in August 1955 he returned to France, saying he planned to spend the rest of the summer in Alsace. This time he would take things more easily. He would rest and recuperate and work on the third volume of his *Philosophy of Civilization*. He might have known he would have little rest. Once again there were to be triumphal tours and once again he was to receive honors from governments, though he had long ago lost faith in their powers to govern.

His affection for England was long-standing. As a student he had wanted to study theology at Oxford; the Oxford theologians had been the first to celebrate the merits of Schweitzer's theological studies. When Queen Elizabeth offered him the highest honor the British Crown could give him, he could hardly refuse. Only one other person outside of Britain has received the Order of Merit. General Eisenhower received it after leading the allied armies to victory. Schweitzer received it because he was supremely a man of peace.

After traveling all night from Alsace he arrived in London on the morning of October 17. He was twenty-four hours before schedule, but the French ambassador heard of his coming and went to the station to greet him. Asked where he was staying, Schweitzer gave the address of a teashop in a part of London called Petty France. For a week this obscure teashop became a place of pilgrimage.

The teashop, kept by an old friend of Schweitzer's, stands close to St. James's Park Tube station. There was the usual glass-sided cash desk, the usual ornate wall-clock and gilt-framed oil-paintings. There was clean table-linen and an air of middle-class respectability. A poster advertised Good Food, Quick Service, Liberal Portions, Pleasant Surroundings. The waitresses sang out their orders and the cash register tinkled. Schweitzer was led to a small back room. It was still early in the morning. He took off his jacket, sat down at the table and began to reply on some cheap notepaper he had brought with him to the letters he carried in the inevitable laundry bag.

He had hoped to spend the morning catching up with his mail, but news of his arrival soon spread, old friends appeared and the tea-shop became a bedlam as everyone craned to see the distinguished visitor in the hand-knitted black cardigan as he sat behind a table littered with manuscripts and letters. A rose-shaded lamp threw a gentle light on his face. He was in jovial mood. "So you have come to see the old ass!" he said to one visitor he had known in

Günsbach. He had trimmed his mustache and cut his shaggy hair which was brushed straight back from the forehead; and in his outmoded clothes, the high wing collar, the severe black tie, he looked like someone from another age.

He remained at the teashop for a week. Most of the time it rained. The smell of cooking invaded the back room, which was separated from the teashop only by a flimsy transparent curtain. To the rattle of crockery, the shouts of waitresses and the clatter of the cash register Schweitzer revised some speeches, wrote letters and received visitors. The greatest in the land came to the teashop to pay him homage—Bertrand Russell the philosopher, Augustus John the artist, Dr. Vaughan Williams the composer. Outside, crowds waited patiently in the rain to catch a glimpse of him. They came to ask advice and to pay tribute, to demand autographs and to take photographs. Some came simply because they wanted to hold his hand. Others came to ask him to give organ recitals. Altogether, there were over 300 requests for organ recitals. The mail came in huge sack-loads. He sighed and tried to catch up with his correspondence, but it defeated him now as it had defeated him before. In Günsbach there is a notice on Schweitzer's door announcing that anyone may enter, but whoever stays more than five minutes is keeping someone else away. To the crowds who came women helpers began to whisper the same advice. An English reporter observed that the tea-shop began to proliferate with women helpers, and some of them had to be removed. Meanwhile the long line of visitors kept moving slowly into the small back room, and Schweitzer dispensed an old-fashioned courtesy to all. Looking astonishingly

young for his years, he talked serenely about Christianity
and Bach and Africa, evading tactfully all the questions he
had no desire to answer, talking in a mixture of French and
German.

In a world which had lost the gift of serenity, he alone
seemed to be serene. Seen from behind the flimsy curtain,
he gave the impression of a ghostly Olympian who had descended for a brief visit to this earth. Close up, he could be
amused, tired, excited, superbly human. His red cheeks
glowed and the neatly combed white hair by the middle of
the week was beginning to grow wild again. Asked what he
thought of the future of Europe, he hunched his shoulders
and said: "My business is ethics, not prophecy. What's the
use of talking about it? Perhaps all the talkers will be top-
pled over in the end." He was in a mood of resignation and
renunciation. To someone who asked him the secret of
repose, he answered: "Appreciate fantasy. When I play my
piano in the evening in Lambaréné I shut my eyes and can
make believe I am playing a great organ and this gives me
true repose." Asked the inevitable question about the English weather, he said: "Oh, one shouldn't worry about
weather. There are far worse things than an English winter."

So it went on, day by day, the streams of visitors, the
whispers of the women helpers, the waitresses shouting:
"Give us another fish fork, ducks!" The Swiss owner of the
tea-shop said by Wednesday: "He is looking tired—there
must be no more visitors." But there was no end to them.
It was the only way the Londoners could offer him tribute.
Nothing quite like this had happened since those long-ago
days when Mahatma Gandhi, wearing sandals and a loin-

cloth, attended the Round Table conference and the Londoners had followed him everywhere, fascinated and awed to have a saint in their midst.

There were brief interruptions to the astounding pilgrimage. He went off to Buckingham Palace to receive the insignia of the Order of Merit. He dined with the Prime Minister in Downing Street. He collected the honorary degree of Doctor of Law from Cambridge University and heard the Orator declare: "Nature has lavished on him all her gifts. He has crowded into one span of life the work and achievement of half a dozen more ordinary men." Then he returned to the back room in Petty France, sat down and corrected more manuscripts, pausing only to look up when a photographer entered or another long line of visitors was formed.

One evening he attended a performance of the London Philharmonic Orchestra, arriving after the interval. He sat in a box while the orchestra played Berlioz's *Symphonie Fantastique*, conducted by Herbert von Karajan. At the end he stood up and applauded, sitting down again quickly when he observed that the eyes of half the audience were on him, not on the conductor. Afterwards, when the hall was empty and the audience had dwindled to a handful of ushers and officials, he sat before the keyboard of the organ. A single stage lamp shone on his bent shoulders as he played —not a Bach prelude, which everyone had expected—but a work by his old friend and teacher, Charles-Marie Widor. The Widor recital came to an end, and then he turned to the *Little Prelude in E Minor*, but he was too tired to complete it and the organ baffled him. It was a large organ with a fantastic number of stops and pipes. Pointing to the pipes, he laughed: "It's like a chemical factory. I'll never learn to play it for a hundred years." The designer of the organ was watching him and looked crestfallen. Schweitzer patted his arm. "Oh, but she is beautiful, truly beautiful," he said. Then he went out into the dark street, where the crowd was clamoring for him to sign concert programs.

When the week-long visit to London came to an end, he was exhausted. There was nothing unusual in this. He had expected it and made preparation for it. He had talked to everyone, delivered himself of brief homilies on Christianity, on tropical medicine, on the state of music, on Bach and Goethe and a hundred other subjects. It was observed that he asked more questions than he answered and resolutely refused the prophetic role people wanted him to assume. He had come very humbly and been received as a hero, and just before leaving London he was asked the inevitable question—why didn't he take a rest? "There's so much to be done," he answered. He was reminded that he would be 81 in a few weeks and was sternly reprimanded for burning the candle at both ends. "You can always burn the candle at both ends if it is long enough," he answered, and went off chuckling. He had given the same answer forty years before.

Once he had said he would retire and develop a taste for sightseeing at the age of 75, but he was still immune from the drug. He visited none of London's famous sights, but looked briefly at some organs, before returning to Günsbach. He usually left Europe for Africa in winter, and whenever possible he liked to spend his birthday in Lambaréné. So on December 16, 1955, after a short four-month visit to

Europe, he embarked for Africa. He spent his eighty-first birthday in Lambaréné; it was a day like all the other days, with no notable decrease in vigor.

Only in one thing had he changed. There had been many occasions when he felt the need for speaking out. At Oslo, at Frankfurt, at Aspen, at Edinburgh he had said what he had to say. Now at last because there was so little time left he preferred silence. When he was asked on his eighty-first birthday whether he had a message to deliver to the world, he answered: "I must not regard myself as a man who is continually talking to the world. I must be humble and silent. This is the best way."

He had studied as few men have studied. He had ranged across the whole field of human knowledge, leaving his seal on everything he touched. He had warned against calamities to come and with astonishing patience he had traced out the causes of the world's tragedy. In a darkening world he had been a beacon of light to all men of good faith, and now there was nothing more to be said.

~~~ 11 ~~~
Portrait of a Hero

THE THICKSET, SLIGHTLY
stooping figure with the mane of unruly hair and the heavy
white walrus mustache still rules the hospital at Lambaréné,
as he ruled it more than forty years ago. Age has not
changed him. He has a stiffness of the knees and does not
walk as often as before, but he retains his magnificent vigor.
He still makes his rounds, still superintends the new building, still cultivates the orchard. He throws his head back
when he laughs in exactly the way that people remember
from forty years ago, and his mood changes with lightning
speed from laughter to the most solemn gravity, and this too
is the same. He still plays the lead-lined piano which was
presented to him by the Bach Society of Paris in 1913. He
is still in process of preparing a complete edition of Bach's
chorales and he is still writing his *Philosophy of Civilization*.
For him time has stood still. He remains—and will remain
to the end—the man who set out from France on March 26,
1913, for an unknown Africa which was so close to his
heart that it never occurred to him to go to any other
place.

But as time goes on the man himself becomes harder to seek. Almost as soon as he arrived in Africa, he was called *nganga*, the witch-doctor. They gave him other names: the chieftain, the heavy one, the tall one. One day a small native girl said he was surely a human leopard, for she had watched him carry a living man to the hospital in the evening and in the morning the man was dead. "He is a white human leopard who is allowed to go about freely," she complained, "while they shut up the black ones in prison." Whenever she saw him, the girl would run away in screaming terror, and though her schoolmistress tried to talk her out of the terror, it was no use. The girl credited him with prodigious and terrible powers. But in fact he did possess those powers: he had power of life and death over the natives of the Ogowe, and to them he was every inch a witch-doctor. The natives who called him *nganga* were perhaps closer to the truth than those who regarded him as a man possessed of the amiable Christian virtues of self-sacrifice and a desire to heal the suffering. If it had been only that, the venture in Africa would not have been worth undertaking.

Stern men, when they become legends, are depicted in the radiance of soft haloes. The ruthless Stalin is shown in innumerable portraits gently patting the heads of little children. The ruthless Schweitzer is shown bending tenderly over a patient in the Lambaréné hospital. To compare Schweitzer with Stalin is to compare the utmost good with the utmost evil, but in these regions opposites meet, or at least they obey the same laws. It is important that we recognize the hard core of Schweitzer's thought. To say he has been ruthless is to underestimate his strength: there was iron in his soul, and tempered steel, and an absolute unyielding faith in his mission. *His mission was nothing less than to revive by his writing and by his example the lost purposes of western civilization.* He gave himself the highest aim known to western man, and if he failed, it was not for lack of energy or of intellectual insight. He failed because western civilization was too far advanced in its unalterable progress, and even the most powerful witch-doctor could not conjure the proper spells to put an end to madness.

In his autobiographical writings Schweitzer has depicted himself outwardly. It is all, or nearly all, on the surface. Only when he speaks of his childhood are we made aware of any attempt to seek the springs of his behavior. He arrives in Lambaréné on such and such a day, there is an epidemic of dysentery, the rain is coming through the roof, the tornadoes are a great misfortune, today there was a difficult operation for strangulated hernia on an old man of the Pahuin tribe. So he goes on, drily recounting for the benefit of his friends in Europe and America the stories of his life in the mission hospital. It is all told with abundant good humor, and there is sometimes a pedagogic gleam in his eyes, as when in *Out of My Life and Thought* he inserts short summaries of his theories on Bach and the Messiahship of Jesus and the nature of the true organ.

What is remarkable is what he leaves out. The force, the pungency, and that element which the mediaeval Italians called *terribilità*, is missing. But at odd intervals in *The Quest of the Historical Jesus, The Mysticism of Paul the*

Apostle and *The Philosophy of Civilization* he reveals himself completely. In those books the long dialogue he has ceaselessly maintained with himself is revealed to the world. It is not a pretty dialogue. He is dealing with fundamental things: things close to the heart of earth and close to the heart of heaven. He says things that shock and wound, and he says them with the authority of a man who knows the effects of shock and wounds. He has little patience with organized Christianity. When he speaks of Christ and St. Paul, he offers for our contemplation figures of imperious majesty, vast and triumphant like the figures which speak out of Byzantine mosaics. And when he contemplates western civilization, he sees the Gadarene swine on their road to perdition. He had no illusions about the fate of civilization. Once, when he was reading on the banks of the Rhine, an insect fluttered between the pages of the book and was almost crushed there. He saved the insect's life, saying: "I am like this poor little thing, in danger of being crushed under the weight of history." He saw no reason why a whole civilization might not vanish as easily as a crushed insect. For him there was only one civilization—the one in which we live: and he cried out against the stupidity of men who, instead of shoring the ruins, seemed determined to destroy their only shelter against barbarism. When he asked men to turn back to the eighteenth century, he was not asking them to turn back the clock. He was asking them to employ the pure light of reason and to uphold the dignity of man, and he was perfectly aware that the French Revolution had perverted human dignity and had destroyed reason by making her into a goddess.

When Schweitzer spoke about the crisis of our time, he spoke with desperate urgency. More than most men, he had advantages of insight. Being both French and German, he was able to penetrate with extraordinary clarity into the motives that lay behind the two poles of European civilization. He found in Lambaréné, one degree below the equator, an almost perfect vantage point for observing the European scene. To the end he remained the European, and found America baffling. Curiously, he was more honored in Sweden and England than in France or Germany. In Lambaréné his chief assistants were Alsatians, Hungarians, Swiss and Dutch. Only one American nurse went out to serve under him.

The strength of Schweitzer lay in his devotion to a single idea—the idea of love. If *Ehrfurcht vor dem Leben* was a vastly richer concept than "reverence for life," he was able to convey the depth of his experience by the simple expedient of showing himself in action. He saw the world *sub specie aeternitatis*. It was very small compared with the flames of the Last Days, which were continually in his mind, but he found the world adorable and he was determined to live the Christian life as he saw it to the end. To live in the world was to live in Christ, and to serve the natives of Africa was at once a terrible duty imposed upon him by the failure of Europe in Africa and a privilege almost too great to be borne.

Though he was a Christian there were times when he despaired of Christianity. He wrote once that he looked forward to a time when there would come a new philosophy, a new ethic, to sustain men's flagging spirits:

I believe there must arise a philosophy profounder and more living than our own, one possessed of greater spiritual and ethical power. In the terrible age through which mankind is passing, all of us, both in the East and the West, must watch for the coming of a more perfect and healthier form of thought which will conquer men's hearts and compel all people to acknowledge its sway. And it must be our aim to bring this philosophy into existence.[1]

It was a sign of his profoundly Christian mind that he could be discontented with Christianity.

Indeed, he was discontented with most things, and that was his virtue. Simply by exiling himself to Lambaréné, he announced his discontent with western civilization, which in his view had already collapsed under the weight of its inhumanity. "Today man pursues his dark way in a time of darkness without freedom or coherence or a cultural sufficiency, having lost himself in his inhumanity and surrendered his spiritual independence and moral judgment to the organized society in which he lives."[2] In Schweitzer's eyes society had long been bankrupt: the tragedy was that there was no receiver in bankruptcy and the debts were continually accumulating.

Again and again he thundered like Jeremiah against the evils at the heart of society, and suffered the usual fate of Jeremiahs: he was praised for his foresight and commended for his integrity, while society continued to follow the disastrous courses of inhumanity without paying heed to his warnings. He inveighed against progress, nationalism, the sub-

[1] *Indian Thought and Its Development.* By Albert Schweitzer. Boston: Beacon Press, 1954.
[2] *The Decay and Restoration of Civilization,* p. 34.

servience of man to his machines. Progress was stifling the spirit, the speeches of nationalists were "the muttering of imbeciles," and the machines were gradually creating a world in which men were becoming enslaved, not only to mechanical ideas, but to the robot precision of machinery itself. In this he was not always on safe ground, for he used mechanical aids in his own hospital, and it is too late in the world's history to turn one's face against machinery.

Above all he wanted a world in which the spirit of man could enjoy its full freedom of development. He wanted a return to simplicity. "The world," he said once," no longer believes the simple can be profound. The spirit of the age loves dissonance." [3] So, with all the strength left in him, he would reiterate the simple profound truths he had derived from his own experience and from the sayings of Jesus. In *The Philosophy of Civilization* he had shown the course western civilization would take, and it had all happened as he expected it would. He had foreseen the rise of Hitler and guessed that emerging Communism with its peculiarly rigid monolithic structure would prove inviting to people who had lost their sense of the freedom of the spirit and were desperate for certainties. The sciences were being studied until the whole earth seemed on the verge of becoming a vast laboratory, but who were studying the pathways of the spirit? The ultimate rules of humanity were being laid aside: men were becoming no more than the servants of perfected instruments of slaughter. They were being led by blind men, and were themselves blind. How many people were studying the human soul and attempting to discover the laws

[3] In a conversation with Stefan Schimanski. *World Review,* June, 1949.

which would bring it to peace and happiness? There were
no more ideals: there was only the implacable state demanding greater and greater power over men. The ideals have
vanished. So he cried out: "Then let us make new ideals and
follow them."

The greatest irony of all was that civilization was in danger of destruction, not from excess of luxury, but from a
deficiency of soul. Nothing quite like this had ever happened
before. It was not in this way that the Roman Empire per-
ished. We perish because the little flame of the spirit is
being blown out. And since organized religion has made its
peace with the state, he finds little hope of a revival of spiritual values through the church. It is odd that the man who is
regarded as the living embodiment of Christianity should
be so hopeless about the services which the church can perform. "In the war," he wrote, "religion lost its purity and
authority by joining forces with the spirit of the world." [4]

So, categorically, Schweitzer announced his opinions,
detesting all kinds of evasions, refusing to submit to relative
ethics when the absolute ethic of Christ lay in front of him.
In a world where relative ethics was a commonplace, his
insistence upon the absolute came like a sudden shock on
exposed nerves to people weary of trivialities. From Leyden
Pastor Robinson wrote to the early Pilgrims in New England after the massacre of Wessagusett that they should
have "that tenderness of the life of man (made after God's
image) which is meet." Schweitzer was doing no more when
he called upon men to have reverence for life, but he spoke
with greater authority than Pastor Robinson possessed.

[4] *Christian Century*, LI, p. 1483.

There, in Africa, in a landscape like a nightmare filled with dark shadows and eerie splashes of light, he showed that reverence for life was a thing of strength and joy, and would prevail. The dying Kurtz screamed of the horror all round him. Schweitzer spoke quietly about reverence, *Ehrfurcht,* a fearful thing, yet so beautiful he could not live without it. There were times in that age of terrible wars and still more terrible concentration camps when he alone seemed to be praising life in all its glory.

"There are no heroes of action," he wrote once. "There are only heroes of resignation and suffering." In their context the words are true, but they are not the whole truth. There is a heroism which goes beyond heroism—into the dark places of the spirit and into the dark landscapes of the earth. Such heroes become terrible ancestors, opening out the virgin lands and summoning men to follow them. Such was Schweitzer, Hero of Africa.

~~~ *Index* ~~~